Edward Sheriff Curtis

Hans Christian Adam

Edward Sheriff Curtis

1868–1952

TASCHEN

HONG KONG KÖLN LONDON LOS ANGELES MADRID PARIS TOKYO

"Your photographs stand by themselves, both in their wonderful artistic merit and in their value as historical documents."

President Theodore Roosevelt in a letter to Edward S. Curtis,
December 16, 1905

»Ihre Photographien sind einzigartig, sowohl in ihrer wunderbaren künstlerischen Qualität, als auch in ihrer Bedeutung als historische Dokumente.«

Präsident Theodore Roosevelt in einem Brief an Edward S. Curtis,
16. Dezember 1905

« Vos photographies sont uniques, tant par leur incroyable qualité artistique que par leur valeur comme documents historiques. »

Le Président Théodore Roosevelt dans une lettre à Edward S. Curtis,
16 décembre 1905

Cañon de Chelly, 1904

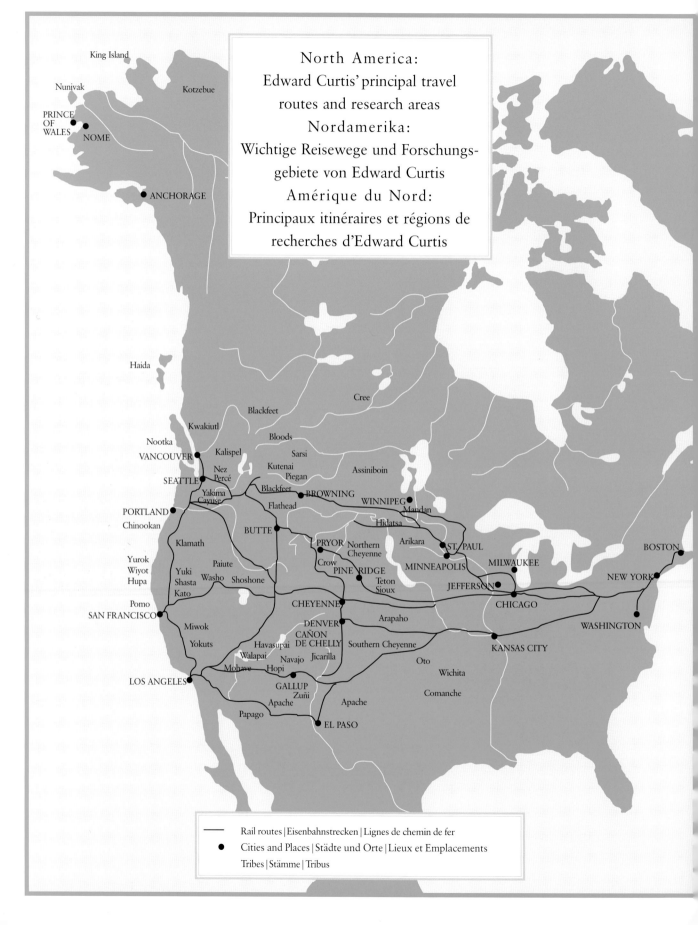

North America:
Edward Curtis' principal travel
routes and research areas
Nordamerika:
Wichtige Reisewege und Forschungs-
gebiete von Edward Curtis
Amérique du Nord:
Principaux itinéraires et régions de
recherches d'Edward Curtis

King Island

Nunivak

Kotzebue

PRINCE
OF
WALES

NOME

ANCHORAGE

Haida

Cree

Blackfeet

Kwakiutl

Bloods

Nootka

Sarsi

VANCOUVER

Kalispel

Kutenai

Assiniboin

Nez
Percé

Piegan

SEATTLE

Blackfeet

BROWNING

WINNIPEG

Mandan

Yakima
Cayuse

Flathead

PORTLAND

Hidatsa

Chinookan

BUTTE

PRYOR

Arikara

ST. PAUL

Klamath

Northern
Cheyenne

Yurok

Paiute

Crow

MINNEAPOLIS

MILWAUKEE

BOSTON

Wiyot

Yuki

PINE RIDGE

Hupa

Shasta

Washo

Shoshone

Teton
Sioux

JEFFERSON

NEW YORK

Kato

CHICAGO

Pomo

CHEYENNE

Arapaho

SAN FRANCISCO

Miwok

DENVER

WASHINGTON

CAÑON
DE CHELLY

Yokuts

Southern Cheyenne

KANSAS CITY

Havasupai

Oto

Walapai

Navajo

Jicarilla

Wichita

LOS ANGELES

Mohave

Hopi

Comanche

GALLUP

Zuñi

Apache

Apache

Papago

EL PASO

────── Rail routes | Eisenbahnstrecken | Lignes de chemin de fer

● Cities and Places | Städte und Orte | Lieux et Emplacements

Tribes | Stämme | Tribus

Contents
Inhalt
Sommaire

8

Portfolio

24

On Edward S. Curtis
Über Edward S. Curtis
A propos d'Edward S. Curtis

Theodore Roosevelt

26

In search of lost time –
Edward S. Curtis and the North American Indian

Auf der Suche nach der verlorenen Zeit –
Edward S. Curtis und die Indianer Nordamerikas

La quête d'une époque révolue –
Edward S. Curtis et les indiens d'Amérique du Nord

Hans Christian Adam

60

Plates
Abbildungen
Illustrations

218

Biography/Bibliography
Biographie/Bibliographie
Biographie/Bibliographie

Captions of the Portfolio | Bildlegenden des Portfolio | Légendes du portfolio

Page | Seite

8   *Black Hair · Plateau, 1900*

9   *Lynx Cap · Navaho, 1905*

10 *Espon Unzo Owa · Mohave, 1903*

11 *Chief Gerónimo · Apache, 1905*
    Häuptling | Le Chef Gerónimo

12 *Apuyótoksi (Yellow Kidney)*
    Piegan, 1910

15 *Two Moons · Cheyenne, 1910*

16 *Red Wing · Apsaroke, 1908*

17 *Sitting Bear · Arikara, 1908*

18 *Bear Bull · Blackfoot, 1926*

19 *Mitat · Wailaki (Athapaska), 1924*

20 *Lone Flag · Atsina, 1908*

23 *Chief Garfield · Jicarilla, 1904*
    Häuptling | Le Chef Garfield

On Edward S. Curtis
Über Edward S. Curtis
A propos d'Edward S. Curtis

Theodore Roosevelt
October I, 1906

Theodore Roosevelt, 1905

In Mr. Curtis we have both an artist and a trained observer, whose pictures are pictures, not merely photographs; whose work has far more than mere accuracy, because it is truthful. All serious students are to be congratulated because he is putting his work in permanent form; for our generation offers the last chance for doing what Mr. Curtis has done. The Indian as he has hitherto been is on the point of passing away. His life has been lived under conditions thru which our own race past so many ages ago that not a vestige of their memory remains. It would be a veritable calamity if a vivid and truthful record of these conditions were not kept. No one man alone could preserve such a record in complete form. Others have worked in the past, and are working in the present, to preserve parts of the record; but Mr. Curtis, because of the singular combination of qualities with which he has been blest, and because of his extraordinary success in making and using his opportunities, has been able to do what no other man has ever done; what, as far as we can see, no other man could do. He is an artist who works out of doors and not in the closet. He is a close observer, whose qualities of mind and body fit him to make his observations out in the field, surrounded by the wild life he commemorates. He has lived on intimate terms with many different tribes of the mountains and the plains. He knows them as they hunt, as they travel, as they go about their various avocations on the march and in the camp. He knows their medicine men and sorcerers, their chiefs and warriors, their young men and maidens. He has not only seen their vigorous outward existence, but has caught glimpses, such as few white men ever catch, into that strange spiritual and mental life of theirs; from whose innermost recesses all white men are forever barred. Mr. Curtis in publishing this book is rendering a real and great service; a service not only to our own people, but to the world of scholarship everywhere.

Mr. Curtis ist beides, Künstler und geübter Beobachter. Seine Aufnahmen sind Bilder, nicht bloß Photographien. Sie besitzen weit mehr als nur Genauigkeit, sie sprechen die Wahrheit. Alle ernsthaften Studenten können sich freuen, denn er bringt jetzt sein Werk in eine dauerhafte Form. Unsere Generation hat als letzte die Chance, das zu tun, was Mr. Curtis getan hat. Der Indianer, wie es ihn heute gibt, stirbt aus. Sein Leben führte er unter Bedingungen, die unsere Rasse schon vor so langer Zeit hinter sich gelassen hat, daß sie vergessen sind. Es wäre eine wirkliche Katastrophe, wenn diese Lebensbedingungen nicht wahrhaftig und lebendig überliefert würden. Doch ein Mann allein kann ein solch umfassendes Bild der Geschichte nicht aufzeichnen. Andere haben in der Vergangenheit daran gearbeitet und tun es noch, um der Nachwelt dieses Dokument zu hinterlassen. Aber Mr. Curtis hat aufgrund einer einzigartigen Kombination von Begabungen, mit denen er gesegnet ist, und in der beeindruckenden Weise, mit der er seine Möglichkeiten zu nutzen verstand, etwas getan, das niemand bisher getan hat; das, soweit wir es beurteilen können, auch niemand außer ihm hätte tun können. Er ist ein Künstler, der im Feld forscht und nicht hinter verschlossenen Türen arbeitet. Er ist ein aufmerksamer Beobachter, dessen geistige und körperliche Fähigkeiten es ihm ermöglichen, seine Beobachtungen vor Ort zu machen, mitten in der Wildnis, die er dokumentiert. Er hat mit vielen verschiedenen Indianerstämmen eng zusammengelebt, in den weiten Ebenen der Prärie, in den Bergen. Er weiß, wie sie jagen, sich fortbewegen, wie sie arbeiten. Er kennt ihre Medizinmänner und Zauberer, ihre Häuptlinge und Krieger, ihre jungen Männer und Mädchen. Er kennt nicht nur ihren rauhen Alltag, sondern hat auch Einblick in ihr so fremdes geistiges und religiöses Leben gewonnen, was wenigen Weißen bisher gelang. Die tiefsten Geheimnisse dieses religiösen Lebens wird nie ein Weißer entschlüsseln können. Mit der Veröffentlichung dieses Buches erweist uns Mr. Curtis einen großen, bedeutenden Dienst, nicht nur unserem eigenen Volk, sondern der Forschung weltweit.

Monsieur Curtis est à la fois un artiste et un observateur expérimenté dont les images sont de véritables compositions et pas simplement des prises de vues ; son travail est beaucoup plus que précis : il est profondément vrai. Quiconque étudie sérieusement doit se féliciter de ce que Monsieur Curtis ait donné à son projet la forme d'une œuvre durable, car c'est à notre génération qu'est offerte la dernière occasion de faire ce qu'il a fait. L'Indien tel qu'il a existé jusqu'ici est sur le point de disparaître. Il a vécu dans des conditions que notre propre race a connues il y a si longtemps qu'il ne nous en reste pas le moindre souvenir. Ce serait un véritable désastre, si l'on ne conservait pas un témoignage vivant et authentique de ces conditions. Aucun homme ne pourrait à lui seul préserver un tel souvenir d'une manière complète. D'autres ont œuvré dans le passé, et œuvrent aujourd'hui encore, pour préserver des parties de souvenir, mais Monsieur Curtis, en raison de la combinaison singulière de ses qualités et de sa faculté extraordinaire à créer et à saisir des opportunités, a été capable de faire ce qu'aucun homme n'avait jamais fait et ce qu'aucun autre homme ne pourrait faire. C'est un artiste qui travaille en plein air et pas entre quatre murs. C'est un observateur attentif, dont les capacités intellectuelles et physiques lui permettent de faire ses observations en pleine nature, au cœur de la vie sauvage qu'il commémore. Il a vécu intimement avec de nombreuses tribus des montagnes et des plaines. Il sait comment elles chassent, comment elles voyagent, comment elles vaquent à leurs diverses occupations, pendant la route ou le campement. Il connaît leurs guérisseurs et leurs sorciers, leurs chefs et leurs guerriers, leurs jeunes hommes et leurs jeunes filles. Il n'a pas seulement vu leur rude existence au grand air, mais a, comme peu d'hommes blancs le feront jamais, saisi de rares aspects de leur étrange vie spirituelle et mentale dont les hommes blancs sont exclus à jamais des recoins les plus secrets. En publiant ce livre, Monsieur Curtis accomplit une grande œuvre, utile non seulement à notre peuple, mais aussi aux chercheurs du monde entier.

In search of lost time

Edward S. Curtis and the North American Indian

Auf der Suche nach der verlorenen Zeit

Edward S. Curtis und die Indianer Nordamerikas

La quête d'une époque révolue

Edward S. Curtis et les indiens d'Amérique du Nord

Hans Christian Adam

Whenever we open a book or magazine or pass a billboard and see an old-fashioned-looking black-and-white photo of a lone "Red Indian" in the wide open prairies, or a chieftain wearing a feather headdress, or a squaw before a tepee, the chances are that the photographer was Edward Sheriff Curtis (1868–1952). His photographic œuvre not only ties in with our traditional idea of the North American Indian, but has largely moulded this idea. Curtis' photographs show Indians as they might once have been – or, rather, as we might wish them to have been.

No other photographer has created a larger body of pictures on this subject. Starting at the turn of the century, Curtis dedicated over thirty years to his goal of capturing the last lived traditions of the Indian tribes in word and image. He spent the greater part of his life studying their life and customs, and noting down their history and their legends, with the result that Curtis the photographer also became an ethnographer.

Many of the remarkable illustrations in this book were taken from the some 2,200 photogravures that Curtis published in the 20-volume encyclopaedia *The North American Indian*, which was the culmination of his many years of endeavour. Originally, this extensive work was to have been printed in a numbered edition of 500. Although it is not known how many copies were actually produced, it can be established that 272 sets of the work were sold at an issue price of 3,000 dollars. The complete title of the encyclopaedia was: *The North American Indian, being a series of volumes picturing and describing the Indians of the United States and Alaska, written, illustrated, and published by Edward S. Curtis, edited by Frederick Webb Hodge, foreword by Theodore Roosevelt, field research conducted under the patronage of J. Pierpont Morgan, in twenty volumes.*

Wenn wir in einem Buch, einer Zeitschrift oder auf einer Plakatwand ein altmodisch wirkendes Schwarzweißphoto sehen, das einen einsamen Indianer in den Weiten der Prärie, einen Häuptling mit Federschmuck oder eine Squaw vor einem Tipi zeigt, dann ist es nicht unwahrscheinlich, daß es sich bei dem Photographen des Bildes um Edward Sheriff Curtis (1868–1952) handelt. Sein photographisches Werk kommt unserer traditionellen Vorstellung von den Indianern Nordamerikas nicht nur entgegen, es hat sie zu einem guten Teil geprägt. Curtis' Photographien zeigen Indianer wie sie einst gewesen sein mögen – oder vielleicht eher, wie wir sie uns gewünscht hätten.

Kein anderer Photograph hat ein größeres Œuvre zu diesem Thema geschaffen. Seit der Jahrhundertwende verfolgte Curtis über 30 Jahre lang das Ziel, die letzten gelebten Traditionen der Indianerstämme in Wort und Bild festzuhalten. Er hat den Großteil seines Lebens damit verbracht, ihr Leben und ihre Gebräuche zu studieren, ihre Geschichte und ihre Legenden zu notieren. Damit wurde der Photograph Curtis auch zum Ethnographen.

Viele der außergewöhnlichen Abbildungen in dem vorliegenden Buch wurden nach den rund 2200 Photogravüren gefertigt, die Curtis als Ergebnis seiner langjährigen Arbeit in der zwanzigbändigen Enzyklopädie *The North American Indian* veröffentlichte. Das umfangreiche Werk sollte ursprünglich in einer numerierten Auflage von 500 Stück gedruckt werden. Wie viele Exemplare fertiggestellt wurden, ist nicht bekannt. Sicher ist, daß 272 Sätze des damals 3000 Dollar teuren Werkes vertrieben wurden, dessen vollständiger Titel lautet: *The North American Indian, being a series of volumes picturing and describing the Indians of the United States and Alaska, written, illustrated, and published by Edward S. Curtis, edited by Frederick Webb Hodge, foreword by Theodore Roosevelt, field research conducted under the patronage of J. Pierpont Morgan, in twenty volumes.*

Die Enzyklopädie ist nicht nur eine der wichtigsten historischen Publikatio-

Quand dans un livre, une revue ou sur des affiches, nous voyons une photo en noir et blanc, à l'air un peu vieillot, qui représente un Indien solitaire au milieu des vastes étendues de la Prairie, un chef coiffé d'une parure de plumes ou une squaw devant un tipi, il n'est pas impossible qu'il s'agisse d'une image du photographe Edward Sheriff Curtis (1868–1952). Non seulement son œuvre photographique a tout pour satisfaire notre vision traditionnelle des Indiens, mais elle l'a même en grande partie conditionnée. Les photographies de Curtis ne montrent pas les Indiens tels qu'ils sont, mais tels qu'ils étaient peut-être autrefois – ou plutôt tels que nous aurions aimé qu'ils soient.

Aucun autre photographe n'a consacré à ce sujet une œuvre d'une telle ampleur. A partir du tournant du siècle, Curtis a poursuivi pendant plus de trente ans l'objectif de fixer par le texte et l'image les dernières traditions vivantes des tribus indiennes. Il a passé la majeure partie de sa vie à étudier leur vie et leurs coutumes et à noter leur histoire et leurs légendes. En ce sens, Curtis photographe a également fait œuvre d'ethnographe.

Un grand nombre des reproductions exceptionnelles qui figurent dans ce livre ont été réalisées à partir des quelque 2200 photogravures que Curtis, au terme de longues années de travail, publia sous la forme d'une encyclopédie en 20 volumes intitulée «The North American Indian». Cette œuvre considérable devait à l'origine faire l'objet d'une édition numérotée tirée à 500 exemplaires. On ignore combien furent en réalité imprimés. Ce qu'on sait, c'est que 272 séries de l'œuvre furent distribuées. Elle coûtait alors 3000 dollars et avait pour titre intégral : *The North American Indian, being a series of volumes picturing and describing the Indians of the United States and Alaska, written, illustrated, and published by Edward S. Curtis, edited by Frederick Webb Hodge, foreword by Theodore Roosevelt, field research conducted under the patronage of J. Pierpont Morgan, in twenty volumes.*

Cette encyclopédie est non seulement l'une des publications historiques les

The encyclopaedia is not only one of the most important historical publications on American Indians, but is also one of the most beautiful books ever produced, an exquisite work printed on heavy paper, leatherbound and with gilt edging. The individual volumes appeared between 1907 and 1930. From 1915, starting with volume X, the words *and the Dominion of Canada* were added to the title, meaning that the entire American continent north of the Mexican border and west of the Mississippi was now covered. Each of the 20 self-contained volumes, which were illustrated with approximately 75 plates measuring 14 x 19 cm (5" x 7") and which featured the occasional chart or map, was dedicated to one or a number of related or topographically contiguous Indian tribes in North America. Placed together, the twenty volumes took up almost a metre and a half of shelf space. Each individual volume was further accompanied by a separate portfolio, which generally contained 36 large-format photogravures, measuring approximately 30 x 40 cm (12" x 16"). These photogravures were also sold in a separate edition of high-quality offprints, and it is especially on these that Curtis' reputation as a photographer rests.

Edward S. Curtis reached the peak of his career, as numerous sources show, between 1905 and 1914. Nevertheless, by the time the last volume of his encyclopaedia appeared in 1930, he was known to only a handful of specialists. On his death in 1952, an obituary in the *New York Times* dedicated all of 76 words to him, referring to his life-work The North American Indian and concluding with the flat statement: "Mr. Curtis was also known as a photographer."[1] It was not until the general revival of interest in the medium of photography in the 1970s that both Curtis' pictures and the photographer himself underwent a renaissance.

nen über Indianer, sondern sie gehört auch zu den schönsten Büchern der Welt, ein exquisites Werk, gedruckt auf schwerem Papier, ledergebunden und mit Goldschnitt versehen. Die einzelnen Bände erschienen zwischen 1907 und 1930. Ab Band X, 1915 wurde dem Titel der Zusatz *and the Dominion of Canada* angefügt. Damit war der gesamte amerikanische Kontinent nördlich der mexikanischen Grenze und westlich des Mississippi abgedeckt. Jeder der 20 in sich abgeschlossenen, mit ungefähr 75 Tafeln im Format von 14 x 19 cm sowie gelegentlich mit Graphiken und Karten illustrierten Textbände war einem oder einer Reihe von verwandten oder topographisch benachbarten Indianerstämmen Nordamerikas gewidmet. Zusammen füllten die Bände knapp eineinhalb Regalmeter.

Eine separate Bildmappe im Portfolioformat, die jeden einzelnen Band begleitete, enthielt in der Regel 36 große Gravüren im Bildformat von ca. 30 x 40 cm. Die darin enthaltenen Photogravüren gelangten auch als Sonderdrucke in den Handel, und besonders auf diesen hochwertigen Drucken beruht Curtis' Ruf als Photograph.

Den Höhepunkt seines Ruhms dürfte Edward S. Curtis, wie zahlreiche Quellen belegen, zwischen 1905 und 1914 erreicht haben. Bei Erscheinen des letzten Bandes seiner Enzyklopädie im Jahr 1930 war er nur noch wenigen Spezialisten bekannt. Als Curtis 1952 starb, widmete ihm die *New York Times* einen kurzen Nachruf von ganzen 76 Worten, in dem an sein Lebenswerk *The North American Indian* erinnert wird und der mit den dürren Worten schließt: »Mr. Curtis war auch als Photograph bekannt.«[1] Erst mit dem allgemeinen Aufleben des Interesses am Medium Photographie in den 70er Jahren unseres Jahrhunderts erlebten seine Bilder und damit auch seine Person eine Renaissance.

Edward Sheriff Curtis wurde 1868 bei Whitewater in Wisconsin auf einer Farm geboren und wuchs nach dem Umzug seiner Familie nach Minnesota

plus importantes sur les Indiens, mais elle figure également parmi les ouvrages imprimés les plus beaux du monde. Il s'agit d'une œuvre de très grande qualité sur beau papier, reliée en cuir et dorée sur tranche. Les volumes parurent un par un entre 1907 et 1930. A partir du volume X (1915), on a rajouté au titre *and the Dominion of Canada*. L'ensemble du continent américain compris entre le nord de la frontière mexicaine et l'ouest du Mississippi était ainsi couvert. Chacun des 20 volumes, formant une unité en soi et illustré d'environ 75 planches de format 14 x 19 cm, ainsi que parfois de cartes et de schémas, était consacré à une ou plusieurs tribus indiennes d'Amérique du Nord unies par des liens de parenté ou proches d'un point de vue topographique. Les volumes réunis remplissaient près d'un mètre et demi de rayonnage. Un portfolio qui contenait en règle générale 36 grandes gravures d'environ 30 x 40 cm, accompagnait chacun des volumes. Ces photogravures étaient également commercialisées sous forme de tirages à part, et c'est principalement l'excellente qualité de leur impression qui valut à Curtis sa réputation de photographe. Ainsi que l'atteste la pluralité des sources, Curtis aurait atteint l'apogée de sa carrière entre 1905 et 1914. Lorsque parut en 1930 le dernier volume de son encyclopédie, il n'était plus guère connu que de quelques spécialistes. A sa mort, survenue en 1952, le *New York Times* lui consacra une courte notice nécrologique qui évoquait l'œuvre de sa vie *The North American Indian* et se terminait sèchement en ces termes : «M. Curtis était également connu comme photographe[1].» Ce n'est qu'avec le regain général d'intérêt que connut le médium photographique dans les années 70 que ses photos, et par là sa personne, connurent un nouvel engouement.

Edward Sheriff Curtis naquit dans un ranch des environs de Whitewater, dans le Wisconsin, en 1868. Suite au déménagement de sa famille dans le Minnesota, il grandit dans une région où vivaient des Indiens Chippewa et Winnebago. L'année de sa naissance est également celle où le chef indien Red

Edward Sheriff Curtis was born in 1868 on a farm near Whitewater, Wisconsin, and, after his family moved to Minnesota, grew up in an area still inhabited at that time by Chippewa and Winnebago Indians. The year of his birth was the year that Chief Red Cloud signed at Fort Laramie the "Peace Treaty" that brought an end to the wars with the Sioux Indians, but which at the same time definitively annulled the autonomous status of the individual tribes, spelling the banishment of the Indians to reservations. Edward's father, the preacher Johnson Curtis, had returned from the Civil Wars as an invalid. Despite this, he went on journeys lasting several days, both on horseback and by canoe, to visit his widely-scattered flock. His son would often accompany him on these trips, and in this way the young Edward became acquainted at an early age with life under the open sky.

Edward Curtis went to school at the local one-room village school, but his formal education came to an end after only six years. Yet he was keen to learn, and he already built his first camera as a young lad after finding the instructions for this in a popular manual that appeared in 1888, *Wilson's Photographics: A series of lessons, accompanied by notes, on all the processes which are needful in the art of photography*. He then acquired the rudiments of photographic technique as an apprentice in a photo studio in St. Paul.

When it proved impossible for Johnson Curtis to continue his strenuous work as a preacher, he settled in 1887 close to Seattle in order to begin a new life. However, he died the very next year, which meant that from now on it was left to Edward, who was just 20 years old at the time of his father's death, to support the family. Edward hired himself out as an occasional agricultural labourer, became a fisherman and clam-digger, and worked at times in a sawmill. But then he saw the possibility of earning money with his photography, and became a partner in a

in einer Gegend auf, in der um diese Zeit noch Chippewa- und Winnebago-Indianer lebten. Sein Geburtsjahr war das Jahr, in dem Häuptling Red Cloud in Fort Laramie den »Friedensvertrag« unterschrieb, der die Indianerkriege der Sioux beendete, zugleich aber den Autonomiestatus der einzelnen Stämme endgültig aufhob und die Vertreibung der Indianer in die Reservate festschrieb. Edwards Vater, der Prediger Johnson Curtis, war als Invalide aus dem Bürgerkrieg zurückgekehrt. Dennoch suchte er seine weit versprengte Gemeinde auf tagelangen Ritten oder per Kanu auf. Sein Sohn, der ihn oft auf Reisen begleitete, lernte so früh das Leben unter freiem Himmel kennen.

Für Edward Curtis endete die Schulausbildung bereits nach dem sechsten Jahr in einer einklassigen Dorfschule. Doch er war wißbegierig und baute bereits als Jugendlicher seine erste Kamera. Die Anleitung dafür fand er in dem populären, 1888 erschienenen Lehrbuch *Wilson's Photographics: A series of lessons, accompanied by notes, on all the processes which are needful in the art of photography*. Professionelle Einweisung in die Technik der Photographie erhielt er dann als Lehrling in einem Photostudio in St. Paul.

Nachdem es ihm nicht mehr möglich war, die anstrengende Arbeit eines Geistlichen zu verrichten, ließ sich Johnson Curtis 1887 in der Nähe von Seattle nieder, um dort ein neues Leben zu beginnen. Er starb jedoch bereits im darauffolgenden Jahr, und von nun an mußte Edward, beim Tod des Vaters gerade 20 Jahre alt, für den Lebensunterhalt der Familie sorgen. Er verdingte sich als Gelegenheitsarbeiter in der Landwirtschaft, war Fischer und Muschelsucher und arbeitete zeitweise in einem Sägewerk. Doch dann sah er die Möglichkeit, mit seiner Photographie Geld zu verdienen, und beteiligte sich an einem Photoatelier, dessen Inhaber er später wurde. Zu erstem Ruhm gelangte er durch sein Talent als Porträtist, und binnen weniger Jahre wurde er zum führenden Gesellschaftsphotographen der Stadt am Pazifik.

Cloud signa à Fort Laramie le «traité de paix» qui mettait un terme aux guerres contre les Indiens Sioux, mais abrogeait définitivement le statut d'autonomie des différentes tribus en même temps qu'il codifiait le bannissement des Indiens dans des réserves. Le père d'Edward, le prédicateur Johnson Curtis, était revenu invalide de la guerre civile. Il parcourait cependant le territoire dispersé de sa paroisse au cours de longs voyages à cheval ou en canoë. Son fils, qui l'accompagnait souvent dans ses tournées, fit ainsi de bonne heure l'expérience de la vie en plein air.

La formation scolaire d'Edward Curtis se termina au bout de seulement six années passées dans une école de village à classe unique. Mais il était animé d'une curiosité d'esprit qui, alors qu'il était encore un adolescent, lui fit fabriquer lui-même son premier appareil photo. Il trouva les instructions dans le manuel populaire Wilson's Photographics : *A series of lessons accompanied by notes on all processes which are needfull in photography,* paru en 1888. Il reçut ensuite une initiation professionnelle dans un studio photo de St. Paul.

Lorsqu'il ne lui fut plus possible d'assumer les contraintes que lui imposaient ses fonctions d'ecclésiastique, Johnson Curtis alla s'installer en 1887 à proximité de Seattle, afin d'y entamer une vie nouvelle. Il mourut cependant dès l'année suivante et Edward, qui était alors âgé de 20 ans, dut subvenir aux besoins de la famille. Il trouva à s'employer comme travailleur saisonnier dans l'agriculture, fut pêcheur et chercheur de coquillages et travailla de façon temporaire dans une scierie. Mais il entrevit bientôt la possibilité de gagner de l'argent avec sa photographie, et il entra dans un studio photographique dont il devint plus tard propriétaire. Ce fut son talent de portraitiste qui lui valut ses premiers succès, et il devint en l'espace de quelques années le premier photographe mondain de cette ville du Pacifique.

Vers 1890, la mode des cartes de visite photographiques, qui impliquaient une grande rapidité d'exécution, était révolue[2] et on s'était tourné vers de

photographic studio, which later came under his sole ownership. His first fame he gained through his talent for portraits, and within a few years he had advanced to become Seattle's leading society photographer.

In the world of photography, quickly produced visiting cards had gone out of fashion by about 1890[2], and people turned to elegant, more extravagant portrait studies. Curtis' studio, which – despite many changes of address over the years – always lay in the heart of the town, produced many imposing works of ladies in evening gowns, children in their Sunday best, marines from the Pacific fleet, and businessmen given to flaunting their success. It is interesting that in many of these commercial studio portraits Curtis' use of lighting is similar to that in his Indian portraits, even if the latter were mostly produced under less easily controlled conditions. However, Curtis also invited some Indians to be photographed in his elegant studio, such as the renowned Chief Joseph of the Nez Percé tribe, who sat for him in 1903. Other famous personalities likewise found their way to Curtis' studio during their stays in Seattle, including the Russian ballerina Anna Pavlova (1881–1931), the Indian writer and winner of the Nobel Prize for literature Rabindranath Tagore (1861–1941), and Jacob Riis (1849–1914), one of the foremost proponents of socio-critical documentary photography.

Curtis would take the portrait of such leading lights in person, while often leaving the day-to-day work to his employees. Consequently a "portrait of a citizen" bearing the angular signature "E. S. Curtis" was not necessarily the work of the photographer. The signature stood rather for the studio and its proprietor.[3] For a long time the studio assured Curtis and his family of their livelihood, so he continued to keep it on even when his interest in Indians grew increasingly important to him.

In der Photographie waren um 1890 die schnell herzustellenden »cartes de visite« aus der Mode gekommen[2], und man hatte sich edlen, aufwendigen Porträtstudien zugewandt. Curtis' Atelier, das mit seinen über die Jahre wechselnden Anschriften stets im Zentrum der Stadt lag, lieferte derartige repräsentative Aufnahmen von Damen in Abendroben, Kindern im Sonntagsstaat, Marinesoldaten der Pazifikflotte und Geschäftsleuten, die ihren Erfolg sichtbar zur Schau trugen. Interessant ist, daß Curtis bei vielen dieser kommerziellen Studioporträts die Beleuchtung ähnlich gesetzt hat wie in seinen Indianerporträts, auch wenn diese meist unter schwerer kontrollierbaren Bedingungen entstanden. Einige der Indianer bat der Photograph aber auch in sein elegantes Studio, um sie dort abzulichten, wie zum Beispiel im Jahr 1903 den berühmten Nez-Percé-Häuptling Joseph.

Auch andere bekannte Persönlichkeiten fanden, während sie sich in Seattle aufhielten, den Weg in Curtis' Studio, darunter die Tänzerin Anna Pawlowa (1881–1931), der 1913 mit dem Literaturnobelpreis ausgezeichnete indische Schriftsteller Rabindranath Tagore (1861–1941) und Jacob Riis (1849–1914), einer der wichtigsten Vertreter der sozialkritischen Dokumentarphotographie. Personen dieses Ranges photographierte Curtis selbst, wohingegen er die Tagesarbeit häufig seinen Mitarbeitern überließ. Daher muß ein »Bürgerporträt«, das die kantige Signatur »E. S. Curtis« trägt, keinesfalls vom Photographen selbst stammen. Der Namenszug auf der Photographie steht für das Atelier und seinen Inhaber.[3] Die Studiotätigkeit sicherte Curtis und seiner Familie lange Zeit den Lebensunterhalt, und so behielt er sie auch bei, als sein Interesse an den Indianern immer stärker wurde.

Nicht weit von seinem Haus am Puget Sound entfernt photographierte Curtis um 1895/96 eines seiner ersten indianischen Modelle. »Prinzessin Angeline« – wie sie von der überwiegend weißen Bevölkerung der Gegend genannt wurde – war die 80jährige Tochter des Häuptlings Sealth, nach dem die Stadt

coûteuses et luxueuses études de portraits. L'atelier de Curtis, qui avait changé plusieurs fois d'adresse au fil des ans, tout en restant dans le centre-ville, produisait des clichés de ce genre où l'on voyait sous leur meilleur jour des dames en robe du soir, des enfants en costume du dimanche, des marins de la flotte du Pacifique et des commerçants soucieux d'afficher leur réussite.

Il est intéressant de noter que dans bon nombre de ces portraits commerciaux réalisés en studio, Curtis a orienté l'éclairage de la même façon que dans ses portraits d'Indiens, lesquels furent réalisés le plus souvent dans des conditions beaucoup plus difficilement maîtrisables. Mais le photographe pria aussi quelques Indiens de se rendre dans son élégant studio pour les y photographier, ainsi le célèbre chef Nez Percé Joseph en 1903.

D'autres personnalités trouvèrent également, durant leur séjour à Seattle, le chemin du studio de Curtis, parmi lesquelles la ballerine Anna Pavlova (1881–1931), le Prix Nobel indien Rabindranath Tagore (1849–1914) et Jacob Riis (1849–1914), l'un des représentants les plus importants de la photographie documentaire comme instrument de critique sociale. Les personnalités de marque étaient photographiées par Curtis lui-même, tandis que le travail quotidien était souvent délégué à des collaborateurs. C'est pourquoi un « portrait bourgeois » portant la signature anguleuse « E. S. Curtis » ne doit aucunement être attribué à la main du photographe. Le paraphe qu'on voyait sur le cliché figurait le studio et ses propriétaires[3]. Le studio assura pendant longtemps les revenus de Curtis et de sa famille, ce qui explique qu'il l'ait conservé à un moment où son intérêt pour les Indiens ne cessait de s'intensifier.

C'est non loin de sa maison située sur le Puget Sound que Curtis photographia, vers 1895–1896, un de ses premiers modèles indiens, la «princesse Angeline», ainsi que la nommait la population, en majorité blanche, de la

Curtis photographed one of his first Indian models around 1895/96 not far from his house at Puget Sound. This was "Princess Angeline," the 80-year-old daughter of Chief Sealth, from whom the city of Seattle took its name. During the following period Curtis went on frequent excursions throughout the environs of Seattle in order to visit and photograph the Indian inhabitants, whose society and culture was still largely intact. Soon afterwards, he put these photographs on sale at his studio.

Around Seattle, Curtis also took numerous landscape photographs. He knew the wilds and the peaks of nearby Mount Rainier so well that he worked there as a mountain guide. In 1898 the photographer was on a short expedition in the mountains when he chanced upon a group of scientists who had lost their way, and brought them back to safety. The encounter was to radically alter his life. Among the scientists were the head of the U.S. Biological Survey, C. Hast Merriam, and the ethnographer and expert on American Indians George Bird Grinnell (1849–1938). The two men showed an interest in Curtis' photographic work and arranged an interesting commission for him. Curtis was able to accompany the Harriman Expedition to Alaska in 1899 as official photographer. The expedition was originally planned as a luxury holiday trip for the railway magnate Edward Harriman. In order to substantiate his reputation as a philanthropist, Harriman had invited some two dozen prominent scientists to join him, including Merriam, Grinnell and the natural historian John Muir. During the journey, Curtis dedicated himself chiefly to landscape photography, producing a number of outstanding glacier shots. Yet the encounter with the scientists and their work had a great influence on him. He participated in the expedition's daily discussions, and in this way did a kind of crash course in the methods and techniques of science.

Seattle benannt war. In der Folgezeit unternahm Curtis häufig Ausflüge in die Umgebung von Seattle, um die dort lebenden Indianer, deren Lebensumfeld noch weitgehend intakt war, aufzusuchen und zu photographieren. Bald darauf verkaufte er diese Aufnahmen bereits in seinem Studio.

In der Umgebung von Seattle machte Curtis außerdem zahlreiche Landschaftsaufnahmen. Die Wildnis und die Gipfel des nahen Mount Rainier kannte er so gut, daß er dort auch als Bergführer arbeitete. 1898 stieß der Photograph während einer kleinen Expedition ins Gebirge zufällig auf eine Gruppe von Wissenschaftlern, die sich verirrt hatte, und brachte diese in Sicherheit. Diese Begegnung sollte sein Leben grundlegend verändern. Unter den Wissenschaftlern befanden sich der Chef des U.S. Biological Survey, C. Hast Merriam, sowie der Ethnograph und Indianerexperte George Bird Grinnell (1849–1938). Die beiden zeigten Interesse an Curtis' photographischen Arbeiten und vermittelten ihm im darauffolgenden Jahr einen hochinteressanten Auftrag.

Als offizieller Photograph konnte Curtis 1899 die Harriman-Expedition nach Alaska begleiten, die ursprünglich als Luxusferienreise für den Eisenbahnmagnaten Edward Harriman geplant war. Um seinen Ruf als Philanthrop zu begründen, hatte Harriman rund zwei Dutzend namhafte Wissenschaftler zur Teilnahme eingeladen, darunter Merriam, Grinnell und den Naturforscher John Muir. Curtis widmete sich während der Reise hauptsächlich der Landschaftsphotographie und schuf einige großartige Gletscheraufnahmen. Doch die Begegnung mit den Wissenschaftlern und ihrer Arbeit hinterließ bei ihm einen tiefen Eindruck. Er nahm an den täglichen Kolloquien der Expedition teil und absolvierte so eine Art Crashkurs zum Thema Techniken und Methoden der Wissenschaft.

Eine weitere Expedition führte Curtis 1900 an der Seite des Ethnographen Grinnell nach Montana, wo er Gelegenheit hatte, unter Indianern zu leben

région. Cette femme âgée de 80 ans était la fille du chef Sealth, qui donna son nom à la ville de Seattle. Curtis entreprit par la suite de fréquentes randonnées autour de Seattle pour y rendre visite aux Indiens autochtones, dont l'environnement était en grande partie intact, et les photographier. Quant à ces photos, il les vendait très peu de temps après dans son studio.

Curtis fit également de nombreuses photos de paysage dans les environs de Seattle. Il connaissait si bien les étendues sauvages et les sommets du Mont Rainier qu'il y travailla comme guide de montagne. Lors d'une petite expédition en 1898, le photographe tomba sur un groupe de scientifiques qui s'étaient perdus, et il les ramena en lieu sûr. Cette rencontre devait changer sa vie de façon radicale. Parmi ces scientifiques se trouvaient le chef de l'U.S. Biological Survey C. Hast Merriam, et l'ethnologue spécialiste des Indiens Bird Grinnell (1849–1938). Les deux hommes se montrèrent intéressés par les travaux photographiques de Curtis et l'aidèrent à obtenir l'année suivante un contrat très intéressant.

En 1899, Curtis put accompagner en tant que photographe officiel l'expédition Harriman en Alaska, qui devait être à l'origine un luxueux voyage touristique destiné au magnat des chemins de fer Edward Harriman. Afin de justifier sa réputation de philanthrope, celui-ci avait invité une bonne vingtaine de chercheurs de renom, parmi lesquels Merriam, Grinnell et le naturaliste John Muir. Pendant la durée du voyage, Curtis se consacra principalement à la photographie de paysage, réalisant quelques photos de glaciers très impressionnantes. Mais sa rencontre avec les scientifiques et leur travail exerça sur lui une grande influence. Participant aux colloques interdisciplinaires qui avaient lieu tous les jours dans le cadre de l'expédition, il suivit ainsi une sorte de cours intensif sur les méthodes et techniques scientifiques.

En 1900, une autre expédition conduisit Curtis, aux côtés du spécialiste des Indiens Grinnell, dans le Montana où il eut l'occasion de vivre parmi des

Into the Desert
Hinaus in die Wüste
Dans le désert
Navaho, 1904

A further expedition in 1900 brought Curtis, in the company of Indian expert Grinnell, to Montana, where he had the opportunity to live among the Indians and photograph them. His visit to the Sun Dance of the Blood, Blackfoot and Algonquin tribes at Browning, Montana, proved to be a second turning point in Curtis' life after the Harrimann expedition, an experience that left a deep impression on him. From now on he devoted himself to learning more about the life of the plains Indians and to capturing them with his camera.

During this expedition, Curtis learnt from Grinnell how to gather scientifically relevant information in a systematic manner. Despite his fascination for the Indians, Curtis knew little about them at first, and initially he shared the whites' prejudice that their religion was nothing but senseless superstition with no deeper meaning. Yet the desire had been kindled in him to learn more about the individual tribes. For his first photographs he asked Indians to restage famous battles or conduct ceremonies for him, attempting to erase all signs of assimilation on the part of the Indians to the culture of the white man. His Indian models, who mostly lived on the reservations, happily posed for Curtis' camera, as if they too wanted to recapture their past – that seemingly carefree everyday existence and that spirituality that the white man had taken from them.

Curtis' activity photographing Indians also proved beneficial to his portrait work back at his studio, and was capable of being used for advertising purposes. The photographer had the thick passe-partout paper for his studio work embossed with an Indian head in profile, set above a tepee and crossed arrows. Photographs of Indians had become the fashion, and now even graced the postcards that the Curtis Studio sold as a side line.[4] A series of postcards showing portraits of Indians and tipis, on sale in Seattle in 1905, bore on the picture side an

und sie zu photographieren. Die Anwesenheit beim Sonnentanz der Blood-, Schwarzfuß- und Algonquin-Stämme bei Browning, Montana, wurde für Curtis nach der Teilnahme an der Harriman-Expedition zum zweiten Schlüsselerlebnis, das ihn tief berührte. Von nun an konzentrierte er sich ernsthaft darauf, mehr über das Leben der Plains-Indianer zu erfahren und es in Photographien festzuhalten. Von Grinnell lernte Curtis während der Expedition, wie man für die Wissenschaft bedeutsame Informationen systematisch sammelt. Trotz aller Begeisterung für die Indianer wußte Curtis anfangs wenig über sie und teilte zunächst das Vorurteil der Weißen, ihre Religion sei ein bedeutungsloser Aberglaube ohne tieferen Sinn. Aber sein Wunsch, mehr über die einzelnen Stämme zu erfahren, war geweckt. Für seine ersten Bilder bat er Indianer, berühmte Schlachten nachzustellen oder Zeremonien vorzuführen, und versuchte, jegliche Zeichen der Anpassung der Indianer an die Kultur des weißen Mannes auszublenden. Seine indianischen Modelle, die meist in Reservaten lebten, posierten gerne für die Photographien, als wollten auch sie damit ihre Vergangenheit wieder einfangen, jenes scheinbar sorgenfreie alltägliche Leben und jene Spiritualität, die ihnen die Weißen genommen hatten. Curtis' Arbeit als Indianerphotograph kam auch dem Porträtgeschäft seines Studios zugute und ließ sich als Werbefaktor nutzen. Den Passepartoutkarton für die Aufnahmen seines Ateliers versah der Photograph mit einem Prägestempel, der einen Indianerkopf im Profil mit gekreuzten Pfeilen und Tipi darunter zeigt. Indianerphotographien waren in Mode gekommen und zierten jetzt auch die Postkarten, die das Curtis-Studio als Nebenerwerb vertrieb.[4] Eine 1905 in Seattle verkaufte Postkartenserie mit Indianerporträts und Tipis weist auf der Bildseite ein freies Textfeld von ungefähr zwei Zentimetern Höhe für Kurzmeldungen auf. Curtis benutzte diese Karten auch zur Eigenwerbung und als Einladungskarten, zum Beispiel für seine meist im Winter gehaltenen Vorträge über Indianer.[5]

Indiens et de les photographier. La présence, pendant la Danse du Soleil, de tribus Blood, Blackfoot et Algonquin dans la région de Browning, Montana, représenta pour Curtis, après sa participation à l'expédition Harriman, une deuxième expérience clé qui le toucha profondément. A partir de ce moment, il concentra son effort sur les Indiens des Grandes Plaines pour en apprendre davantage sur leur vie et la fixer dans des photographies. Durant l'expédition, Curtis apprit de Grinnell comment collecter de façon systématique des informations porteuses de valeur scientifique. Malgré toute la fascination qu'il éprouvait pour les Indiens, Curtis à ses débuts ne connaissait que peu de choses sur eux, et il partageait le préjugé des Blancs qui voyaient dans leur religion de la simple superstition. Mais son désir d'en apprendre davantage sur les différentes tribus était éveillé. Pour ses premières images, il demanda à des Indiens de refaire les réglages de batailles célèbres ou de figurer des cérémonies, et s'efforça de faire disparaître tout signe qui aurait pu témoigner de l'adaptation des Indiens à la culture de l'homme blanc. Ses modèles indiens, qui vivaient le plus souvent dans des réserves, posaient volontiers pour les photographies, comme s'ils voulaient eux aussi se réapproprier leur passé, cette existence quotidienne apparemment insouciante et cette vie spirituelle que les Blancs leur avaient prises. Le travail photographique de Curtis sur les Indiens fut également utile à ses affaires et à son activité de portraitiste de studio. Le photographe en fit un usage publicitaire en apposant sur le passe-partout en carton dont il encadrait les clichés de son atelier une estampille représentant une tête d'Indien de profil avec des flèches croisées et un tipi. Les photos d'Indiens étaient devenues à la mode et ornaient également les cartes postales dont la diffusion assurait à présent au studio Curtis des revenus annexes[4]. Une série de cartes vendues à Seattle en 1905 et montrant des portraits d'Indiens et des tipis, présente au recto de l'image une marge blanche d'environ deux centi-

empty space approximately two centimetres high for brief messages. Curtis used these cards also for advertising and as invitations, for example to his lectures on the Indians, which he mostly delivered in the winter.[5]

Slowly but surely Curtis' national reputation as a photographer of Indians grew. From 1896 onwards, he was awarded numerous prizes by the National Geographical Convention for his romantic idealized Indian pictures, such as his silhouette of a woman bent down and searching for clams before a picturesque sunset. In 1896 he also received a prize from the Photographers' Association of America, of which he was a member.

The idea of creating an extensive documentation of the traditional ways of the vanishing Northern American tribes came to Curtis around 1903. Since the turn of the century, he had been photographing numerous Indians in the western states, visiting groups in the south-west, and gaining a broad outline of the range of topics that he was to focus on in his later publications. Looking back, it is evident that the Indian photographs he took prior to about 1904 were preliminary studies for his great work *The North American Indian*, whose concept now gradually took shape.

Curtis conceived of the plan systematically to capture in word and image the history of all of the Indian tribes, their life, ceremonies, legends and myths. The areas he wished to investigate were language, social and political organization, geographical context, living conditions, dress, procurement and preparation of food, religious customs, the rituals and customs pertaining to birth, marriage and death, as well as games, music and dance, and even weights and measures. He studied all these areas thoroughly and with a passion for detail. But his most significant contribution was in the hitherto little researched field of mythology and religion.

Curtis nationaler Ruf als Indianerphotograph wuchs langsam und beständig. Die National Photographic Convention zeichnete ihn ab 1896 mehrfach für seine romantisch verklärten Indianerbilder mit Preisen aus, so zum Beispiel für die Silhouette einer gebückten Muschelsammlerin vor einem malerischen Sonnenuntergang. Auch die Photographers' Association of America, deren Mitglied Curtis war, verlieh ihm 1896 einen Preis.

Die Idee, eine umfangreiche Dokumentation über das traditionelle Leben der aussterbenden Indianerstämme Nordamerikas zu schaffen, hatte Curtis um 1903. Bereits seit der Jahrhundertwende photographierte er zahlreiche Indianer in den westlichen Staaten, besuchte Stämme im Südwesten und verschaffte sich einen Überblick über das Themenspektrum, mit dem er sich in seinen späteren Veröffentlichungen genauer beschäftigen sollte. Im Rückblick wird deutlich, daß seine bis etwa 1904 entstandenen Indianerbilder Vorstudien zu dem großen Werk *The North American Indian* waren, dessen Konzept nun langsam Gestalt annahm.

Curtis faßte den Plan, die Geschichte aller Indianerstämme, ihr Leben, ihre Zeremonien und ihre tradierten Legenden und Mythen systematisch in Wort und Bild festzuhalten. Die Bereiche, die er untersuchen wollte, waren Sprache, soziale und politische Organisation, geographisches Umfeld, Wohnverhältnisse, Kleidung, Nahrungsmittelbeschaffung und -zubereitung, Maße und Gewichte, religiöse Bräuche sowie Sitten und Zeremonien bei Geburt, Ehe und Tod, ferner Spiele, Musik und Tänze. All diese Themen erforschte er gründlich und mit Liebe zum Detail, wo und wann immer es die Umstände zuließen. Seinen wichtigsten Beitrag aber leistete er auf dem zuvor wenig erforschten Gebiet von Mythologie und Religion.

Zur Umsetzung seines Plans begann Curtis eine rege Reisetätigkeit; bis 1928 besuchte er mehr als 80 Indianerstämme. Um seiner selbstgestellten Aufgabe gerecht zu werden, mußte der Photograph von Anfang an und über viele Jahre bei Hitze und Kälte, extremer Trockenheit und Schnee photographie-

mètres de large, sur laquelle on pouvait écrire un message. Curtis utilisait également ces cartes pour sa propre publicité et comme cartons d'invitation, par exemple pour ses conférences sur les Indiens, qu'il tenait le plus souvent en hiver[5]. La réputation nationale que se fit Curtis avec ses photos d'Indiens connut une lente et constante progression. La National Photographic Convention lui décerna à partir de 1896 plusieurs prix pour la transfiguration romantique dont il nimbait ses photos d'Indiens, comme par exemple la silhouette courbée d'une chercheuse de coquillages se détachant sur un pittoresque coucher de soleil. La Photographers' Association of America, dont il était membre, lui attribua elle aussi un prix en 1896.

L'idée de créer une vaste documentation sur la vie traditionnelle des tribus indiennes en voie de disparition date d'environ 1903. En photographiant de nombreux Indiens des Etats de l'Ouest et en rendant visite à des tribus du Sud-Ouest, Curtis se fit dès le tournant du siècle une idée d'ensemble des thèmes qu'il devait par la suite examiner plus en détail dans ses publications. Il apparaît nettement avec le recul que les photos qu'il fit des Indiens jusqu'en 1904 environ étaient des études préalables à sa grande œuvre *The North American Indian*, dont le concept avait lentement pris forme.

Le projet de Curtis consistait à fixer systématiquement par le texte et l'image l'histoire de toutes les tribus indiennes, leur vie, leurs cérémonies, leurs légendes et leurs mythes. Les domaines qu'il voulait interroger étaient la langue, l'organisation sociale et politique, le milieu géographique, l'habitat, les vêtements, l'approvisionnement et la préparation de la nourriture, les traditions religieuses ainsi que les us et coutumes relatifs à la naissance, au mariage et à la mort, auxquels s'ajoutaient les jeux, la musique et les danses ainsi que les poids et mesures. Chaque fois que l'endroit et le moment le permettaient, il consacrait à tous ces thèmes des recherches minutieuses qui faisaient preuve d'un grand amour du détail. Mais son apport essentiel concernait les thèmes de la mythologie et de la religion.

In order to realize his plan, Curtis embarked upon an intense period of travel, visiting in the years up to 1928 more than eighty Indian tribes. To do justice to his self-imposed task, he had from the outset and for years on end to photograph in both heat and cold, in drought conditions and in snow. As one of his friends put it, he "exchanged ease, comfort, home life, for the hardest kind of work, frequent and long continued separation from his family, the wearing toil of travel through difficult regions, and finally the heart-breaking struggle of winning over to his purpose primitive men, to whom ambition, time and money mean nothing, but to whom a dream or a cloud in the sky, or a bird flying across the trail from the wrong direction, means much."[6]

As a result of both his ignorance and inquisitiveness, Curtis at first unwittingly broke a number of unwritten laws during his research expeditions, and was correspondingly coolly received by the Indians. He was ambushed and shot at, and on one occasion an Indian threw a handful of earth at his camera. The culprit was highly surprised when Curtis drew a knife and leapt at him, to the applause of the onlooking Indians. This behaviour also accords with the description of Curtis' character that we have from one of his contemporaries: he was "a robust, genial artist, of virile and courageous proportions [... he was], strong both in courage and physical vigour. [... He was] an undisputed genius. His artistic conceptions were blended with imagination, intuition and sound organizational skill."[7]

During his early fieldwork, the photographer required the assistance of an interpreter, who would generally be an Indian from the tribe in question. Although with time Curtis learned a number of Indian languages, it seemed to him advantageous – not least in view of his early blunders – to have a member of the tribe at his side

ren. Er mußte, so einer seiner Freunde, »die Bequemlichkeit des häuslichen Lebens aufgeben, die härteste nur vorstellbare Arbeit, häufige und lange Abwesenheiten von zu Hause ertragen und sich der Mühsal aussetzen, immerfort durch schwieriges Gelände zu reisen. Schließlich mußte er sich der zermürbenden Überzeugungsarbeit widmen, die Indianer für seine Aufgabe zu gewinnen: Menschen, für die persönliches Vorwärtskommen, Zeit und Geld nichts, hingegen aber ein Traum, eine Wolke am Himmel oder ein Vogel, der aus der falschen Richtung den Weg überfliegt, sehr viel bedeuten.«[6]

Aufgrund seiner Neugierde und Unwissenheit übertrat Curtis während seiner Forschungsreisen anfangs ungewollt manch ungeschriebenes Gesetz und wurde von den Indianern entsprechend kühl aufgenommen. Es wurde aus dem Hinterhalt auf ihn geschossen, und einmal warf ein Indianer mit einer Handvoll Erde nach seiner Kamera. Der Missetäter war sehr überrascht, als Curtis ein Messer zog und auf ihn zusprang, woraufhin die umstehenden Indianer Beifall spendeten. Dieses Verhalten entspricht der Beschreibung seines Charakters durch einen Zeitgenossen: Curtis sei ein »widerstandsfähiger, genialer Künstler von Format – männlich und mutig. Tapferkeit und Körperkraft geben ihm Stärke, und zweifellos ist er hoch begabt. Seine künstlerischen Ideen sind eine Mischung aus Phantasie, Einfühlungsvermögen und Organisationstalent«.[7]

Für seine frühen Feldstudien benötigte der Photograph einen Übersetzer, meist einen Indianer des betreffenden Stammes. Obwohl Curtis im Laufe der Zeit mehrere Indianersprachen erlernte, erschien es ihm – auch angesichts der frühen Mißgeschicke – vorteilhaft, ein Mitglied des Stammes als Berater und Vertrauten an seiner Seite zu haben. Mit der Zeit gewann Curtis das Vertrauen und die Freundschaft der Indianer, die ihn zunehmend als Chronisten ihrer Traditionen schätzten. »Der Mann, der auf seinem Atem schläft«, nannten ihn die Hopis, nachdem sie gesehen hatten, wie er seine Luftmatratze aufblies.[8]

Dans la perspective de réaliser son grand projet, Curtis se mit à développer une intense activité de voyageur et, jusqu'en 1928, il rendit visite à plus de 80 tribus différentes. Afin de satisfaire à la tâche qu'il s'était lui-même fixée, le photographe dut dès le début et pendant de nombreuses années travailler sous la chaleur et dans le froid, dans la sécheresse et sous la neige. Il dut, comme le rapporte un de ses amis, «abandonner le confort de la vie domestique pour le travail le plus dur que l'on puisse imaginer, pour les absences, à la fois longues et répétées, loin de chez lui, s'exposant à la fatigue de voyages incessants à travers des régions difficiles. Il lui fallait pour finir déployer des trésors de persuasion pour gagner les Indiens à sa cause, des hommes pour qui l'ambition, le temps et l'argent ne signifient rien, mais pour qui un rêve, un nuage dans le ciel ou un oiseau qui survole le chemin dans la mauvaise direction veulent dire beaucoup de choses[6]».

Durant ses expéditions, la curiosité et l'ignorance de Curtis lui firent involontairement transgresser des lois coutumières, ce qui lui valut un accueil froid de la part des Indiens. On tira sur lui au cours d'une embuscade et un jour, un Indien lança une poignée de terre sur son appareil photo. Le malfaiteur fut très surpris de voir Curtis tirer un couteau et se précipiter sur lui, acte qui recueillit les applaudissements des Indiens assistant à la scène. La description que fit un contemporain du caractère de Curtis va elle aussi dans le sens de ce type de comportement. Selon lui, Curtis était un «artiste génial et endurant, doué d'une envergure, d'une vaillance et d'une force qui s'appliquent tout autant à son courage qu'à son physique, et qui fait preuve de véritables traits de génie. Ses idées artistiques sont un mélange d'imagination et d'inspiration, doublées d'un grand talent d'organisateur[7]».

Pour ses premières études sur le terrain, le photographe eut besoin d'un interprète. Même si Curtis, au fil du temps, apprit les langues de plusieurs tribus, il lui semblait judicieux, ne serait-ce que par rapport aux mésaventures de ses débuts, d'avoir à ses côtés un membre de la tribu.

as an adviser and informant. Over the years Curtis won the trust and friendship of the Indians, who for their part came increasingly to appreciate him as the chronicler of their traditions. He was "the man who sleeps on his breath," as the Hopi called him after watching him inflate his airbed.[8]

In 1911 Curtis mentioned to a reporter from the *New York Times* that many of the tribes were not only willing to help him in his project, but were even anxious to do so. They had grasped the idea that his undertaking was to be a permanent memorial to their life and tradition. "A tribe that I have visited and studied lets another tribe know that, after the present generation has passed away, men will know from this record what they were like, and what they did, and the second tribe does not want to be left out."[9] Towards the end of his project, Curtis reported that tribes which for years he had vainly tried to contact had sent word that they would now be glad to receive him. They had realized that their traditions were purely oral, and that Curtis was the only person who was interested in their traditions and who wished to preserve these traditions in word and picture. He noted down everything that they divulged to him and which he and his assistants observed.

Although Curtis' Indian pictures were already well-known shortly after the turn of the century, he was unable to fund his ambitious documentary project solely from the sales of his photographs. Thus it was an extremely fortunate circumstance that president Theodore Roosevelt should come to know of his work and support the photographer. Erastus Brainerd, a prominent local politician from Seattle, had shown the president a collection of Curtis' Indian pictures during a visit to Washington, and the president had reacted with enthusiasm, relaying to Curtis that he regarded his photographs as very important. Yet direct contact between the photo-

1911 erwähnte Curtis gegenüber einem Reporter der *New York Times*, daß viele Stämme nicht nur willens seien, bei seinem Projekt mitzuarbeiten, sondern sogar sehr großen Wert darauf legten, ihn zu unterstützen. Sie hätten die Idee verstanden, daß seine Unternehmung der dauerhaften Erinnerung an ihr Leben und ihre Traditionen diene. »Ein Stamm, den ich besucht und studiert habe, läßt einen anderen wissen, nachdem die heutige Generation ausgestorben ist, würden die Menschen aus meinen Büchern erfahren, wie die Indianer gelebt haben. Der zweite Stamm möchte da nicht nachstehen.«[9] Gegen Ende seines Projekts berichtete Curtis, Stämme, die er seit Jahren vergeblich zu kontaktieren versucht hatte, hätten ihn informiert, daß sein Besuch nun willkommen sei. Es war ihnen bewußt geworden, daß ihre Überlieferungen allein mündlicher Art waren und daß Curtis der einzige war, der sich für ihre Traditionen interessierte und diese in Wort und Bild festhalten wollte. Er notierte alles, was sie ihm mitteilten und was er und seine Mitarbeiter beobachteten.

Obwohl Curtis' Indianerbilder kurz nach der Jahrhundertwende bereits sehr bekannt waren, vermochte der Photograph sein anspruchsvolles Dokumentationsprojekt mit dem Verkauf von Photographien nicht selbst zu finanzieren. So erwies es sich als äußerst glücklicher Umstand, daß Präsident Theodore Roosevelt Curtis' Arbeiten kennenlernte und den Photographen förderte. Als Erastus Brainerd, ein prominenter Lokalpolitiker aus Seattle, während eines Besuches in Washington dem Präsidenten eine Sammlung von Curtis' Indianerbildern zeigte, war dieser begeistert und ließ Curtis mitteilen, daß er seine Aufnahmen für sehr bedeutsam halte. Der direkte Kontakt zum Präsidenten kam dann jedoch auf einem anderen Weg zustande. Die Zeitschrift *Ladies' Home Journal* prämierte 1904 bei einem Photowettbewerb die zwölf schönsten Kinderphotos der USA, und unter den 18 000 Einsendungen gewann Curtis' Porträt des Mädchen Marie Fischer aus Seattle

Avec les années, Curtis gagna la confiance et l'estime des Indiens qui le considéraient de plus en plus comme le chroniqueur de leurs traditions. «L'homme qui dort sur son souffle», c'est ainsi que l'appelaient les Indiens Hopi après l'avoir vu gonfler son matelas pneumatique[8].

Curtis rapporta en 1911 à un reporter du *New York Times* que de nombreuses tribus avaient non seulement l'intention de collaborer à son projet, mais qu'elles attachaient même beaucoup d'importance à le soutenir dans sa tâche. Elles avaient compris que son entreprise servait la mémoire de leur vie et de leurs traditions. «Une tribu à laquelle j'ai rendu visite et que j'ai étudiée fait savoir à une autre qu'après la disparition de la génération actuelle, les gens apprendront grâce à mes livres comment les Indiens ont vécu. Il s'ensuit que la seconde tribu ne voudrait pas être de reste[9].» Vers la fin de son entreprise, Curtis rapporta que des tribus qu'il avait en vain essayé de contacter depuis des années lui firent savoir que sa visite serait à présent la bienvenue. Elles avaient pris conscience du fait que, leurs traditions étant exclusivement orales, Curtis était à cette époque le seul à s'y intéresser et à vouloir les transcrire. Il notait tout ce qu'elles lui communiquaient, ainsi que les observations que luimême et ses collaborateurs recueillaient.

Même si, peu de temps après le tournant du siècle, ses photos d'Indiens étaient déjà très connues, Curtis n'était pas en mesure de financer lui-même son ambitieux projet documentaire par la vente de ses clichés. Aussi la découverte de ses travaux par le président Theodore Roosevelt et le soutien que celui-ci apporta au photographe firent-ils figure de concours de circonstances on ne peut plus heureux. Lorsqu'au cours d'une visite à Washington, Erastus Brainerd, homme politique de premier plan originaire de Seattle, montra une collection de photos d'Indiens de Curtis au président, celui-ci se montra enthousiaste et fit savoir au photographe qu'il considérait ses clichés comme très importants. Mais le contact direct avec le président se fit par une

grapher and the president came to be established by a somewhat different route. In 1904 the *Ladies' Home Journal* gave an award for the twelve most beautiful photos of children taken in the USA, and Curtis' portrait of Marie Fischer of Seattle won first prize out of 18,000 entries. After its publication, Curtis received a commission from Theodore Roosevelt and his wife to photograph the first family, and was invited to their holiday home Sagamore Hill on Long Island.[10]

Curtis later described his stay at Sagamore Hill: "I had brought along about 100 large-format Indian pictures and Theodore Roosevelt spent much time looking them over. The more he looked, the more enthusiastic he became. I told him of my hopes and plans for spending a part of each summer with the Indians until I had covered all the important tribes. The President slapped me on the back and said, 'Bully for you. I am delighted that you are planning to do that.' His vision of the importance of making such a record of the Indians was far beyond anything I had dreamed of."[11] The president, who regarded himself as one of the last of the "frontiersmen" of the American continent, may well have been reminded of his youth while looking at Curtis' photos. He was very keen to see the old picture of the West preserved, complete with Indians. Theodore Roosevelt promised to write a foreword for the projected publication, and with that gave his semi-official blessing to Curtis' work on the planned *magnum opus*.

At the suggestion of the president's sister, Mrs Douglas Robinson, who already knew Curtis' photographs from an exhibition she had seen in Washington, the photographer exhibited his work in the same year in New York's Waldorf Astoria Hotel. The sepia photographs, hung on velvet drapes, were atmospherically lit, and in an

den ersten Preis. Nach der Veröffentlichung des Bildes erhielt der Photograph von Theodore Roosevelt und seiner Frau den Auftrag, die Präsidentenfamilie zu porträtieren, und wurde dafür auf den Ferienwohnsitz Sagamore Hill auf Long Island eingeladen.[10]

Curtis berichtete über diesen Aufenthalt in Sagamore Hill: »Ich hatte ungefähr 100 großformatige Indianerphotographien mitgebracht, und zwischen den Porträtsitzungen verbrachte Theodore Roosevelt längere Zeit damit, sie zu betrachten. Je länger er sie ansah, desto enthusiastischer wurde er. Ich berichtete von meinen Plänen, jedes Jahr einen Teil des Sommers bei den Indianern zu verbringen, und zwar so lange, bis ich alle wichtigen Stämme besucht hätte. Der Präsident klopfte mir ermutigend auf den Rücken und sagte: ›Toll, ich bin hocherfreut, daß Sie das tun wollen.‹ Seine Vorstellung von der Bedeutung einer solchen Dokumentation der Indianer reichte viel weiter, als ich mir erträumt hatte.«[11] Der Präsident, der sich für einen der letzten Pioniere des amerikanischen Kontinents hielt, hatte sich bei der Betrachtung von Curtis' Photographien möglicherweise an seine Jugendtage erinnert gefühlt. Das Bild des Westens einschließlich der Indianer wollte er festgehalten sehen. Theodore Roosevelt versprach, ein Vorwort für die geplante Publikation zu schreiben, und segnete damit die Arbeiten zu Curtis' geplantem *opus magnum* ab.

Auf Anregung der Schwester des Präsidenten, Mrs. Douglas Robinson, die Curtis' Bilder bereits auf einer Ausstellung in Washington gesehen hatte, stellte der Photograph im selben Jahr im New Yorker Waldorf-Astoria-Hotel aus, wo seine sepiagetönten Photos stimmungsvoll beleuchtet auf samtener Wandbespannung zu sehen waren. Im benachbarten Saal hielt Curtis täglich Vorträge über sein Projekt. Mit der Ausstellung hatte sich Curtis in Unkosten gestürzt, doch der Einsatz lohnte sich. Die Kritiken fielen positiv aus, und schon am zweiten Öffnungstag waren alle Bilder verkauft. Illustre Mitglie-

tout autre voie. Un concours photo organisé en 1904 par la revue *Ladies' Home Journal* devait récompenser les 12 plus belles photos d'enfants des Etats-Unis. Parmi les 18 000 envois, c'est le portrait par Curtis d'une jeune fille de Seattle, Marie Fischer, qui reçut le premier prix. A la suite de la publication de cette photo, Theodore Roosevelt et son épouse passèrent commande au photographe d'un portrait de la famille présidentielle, et l'invitèrent à cet effet dans leur résidence secondaire de Sagamore Hill, à Long Island[10].

Curtis rapporta à propos de son séjour à Sagamore Hill : « J'avais apporté une centaine de photographies d'Indiens grand format, et entre les séances de pose, Theodore Roosevelt passa un long moment à les regarder. Plus il les regardait, plus il se montrait enthousiaste. Je lui parlai de mon intention de passer tous les ans une partie de l'été avec les Indiens, et cela aussi longtemps qu'il me serait nécessaire pour rendre visite à toutes les tribus importantes. Le président me tapa dans le dos en signe d'encouragement et dit : ‹ Formidable, je suis enchanté que vous vouliez faire cela. › L'idée qu'il se faisait de la signification qu'aurait cette entreprise allait beaucoup plus loin que tout ce que j'aurais pu imaginer[11]. » Il est possible que le président, qui se considérait comme l'un des derniers pionniers du continent américain, se soit souvenu de sa jeunesse en regardant les photographies de Curtis. Il tenait à ce que l'on retienne l'image de l'Ouest avec les Indiens. Theodore Roosevelt promit d'écrire une préface pour la publication et accorda ainsi semi-officiellement sa bénédiction au grand projet de Curtis.

Suivant la suggestion de la sœur du président, Madame Douglas Robinson, qui avait déjà vu les images de Curtis à une exposition à Washington, le photographe exposa cette année-là à l'hôtel new-yorkais Waldorf Astoria. On pouvait y voir, fixées sur des tentures murales de velours, ses photos aux tons sépia savamment mises en valeur par l'éclairage, tandis que la pièce

adjacent room Curtis held daily lectures on his project. He had gone to a lot of expense for the exhibition, but it paid off. The reviews were positive, and by the second day the entire stock of photographs was sold out. Illustrious names from New York's high society such as Mrs John Pierpont Morgan, Mrs Frederick Vanderbilt, Mrs Stuyvesant Fish and Mrs Douglas Robinson had pinned their calling cards to the frames to signal their intention to buy.[12]

From this point on the photographer gave numerous lantern-slide lectures and wrote articles for a variety of magazines and newspapers. In short, he did a large amount of public relations work in order to fund his project, which was a rare activity for a photographer. Whenever he rubbed shoulders with high society, he revealed himself to be a charming socialite with keen repartee. Yet he preferred to present himself as an adventurer, dressed in a wild-west outfit and floppy hat. It is with this look that the photographer passed himself off in a self-portrait which he so avidly handed out for inclusion in every conceivable publication that he immediately had it printed in a large edition as a photogravure.

A contemporary described the photographer's appearance as follows: "He is a funny fellow to look at. He is sort of tall and angular. He wears a thin black tie, tied carelessly, while he always has a hat on his head that looks as though it had been run over by a train … He has a dreamy sort of a drawly voice. His blue eyes are sleepy ones, with a half subdued air of humour lurking in their depths. He never smiles with his lips; lips were made for talking. He is never in a hurry. And right there is where he fools 'em. He can work. He tears it off by the yard. During working hours he's a regular business end of a Kansas cyclone. He can outride the Indians and out-

der der gehobenen New Yorker Gesellschaft wie Mrs. John Pierpont Morgan, Mrs. Frederick Vanderbilt, Mrs. Stuyvesant Fish und Mrs. Douglas Robinson hatten ihre Visitenkarten an die Rahmen der Bilder geheftet, um ihr Kaufinteresse zu dokumentieren.[12]
Curtis hielt von nun an viele Lichtbildvorträge und publizierte Artikel in zahlreichen Zeitungen und Zeitschriften. Um sein Projekt zu finanzieren, leistete er eine umfangreiche, für einen Photographen ungewöhnliche Öffentlichkeitsarbeit. Bei seinen Auftritten in der High-Society erwies er sich als charmanter, locker plaudernder Salonlöwe. Lieber jedoch präsentierte er sich als Abenteurer im Wild-West-Look mit Schlapphut. So zeigt ihn ein Selbstporträt, das er so häufig zum Abdruck in allen nur denkbaren Publikationen verteilte, daß er es gleich in größerer Auflage als Photogravüre herstellen ließ. Ein Zeitgenosse beschreibt Curtis' Erscheinungsbild wie folgt: »Er ist ein lustiger Bursche, wenn man ihn so betrachtet […]. Er ist groß und ein bißchen eckig. Er trägt eine dünne, schwarze, sorglos geknotete Krawatte und hat immer einen Hut auf, der aussieht, als wäre er von der Straßenbahn überfahren worden […]. Er hat eine träumerische, sonore Stimme […]. Seine blauen Augen blicken schläfrig, mit einem Funken unterdrückten Humors […]. Seine Lippen zeigen nie ein Lächeln. Lippen sind zum Reden gemacht. Er hat es nie eilig. Und genau hier schätzt man ihn falsch ein. Er kann arbeiten, ja, er reißt sich die Beine aus. Während seiner Arbeitszeit rauscht er umher wie ein Zyklon. Er kann schneller reiten als jeder Indianer und hält, wenn es unbequem wird, noch mehr aus als sie.«[13] Edward Sheriff Curtis wurde zu einer Person des öffentlichen Lebens, und seine zahlreichen Aktivitäten mehrten seinen Ruf, und doch standen die Einnahmen, die er als Photograph erzielte, nach wie vor nicht in einem angemessenen Verhältnis zu seinen Kosten. Um seine Pläne organisatorisch und publizistisch umsetzen zu können, bat Curtis 1906 den Eisenbahnmagnaten und Finanzier John Pierpont Morgan

voisine était réservée aux conférences que Curtis tenait quotidiennement sur son projet. Cette exposition avait certes coûté de l'argent à Curtis, mais l'enjeu en valait la peine. Les critiques furent positives et deux jours après l'ouverture, tout le stock de photos était vendu. Des membres éminents de la haute société new-yorkaise comme Mesdames John Pierpont Morgan, Frederick Vanderbilt, Stuyvesant Fish et Douglas Robinson avaient épinglé leurs cartes de visite sur les cadres des images pour manifester leur intérêt et leur intention d'achat[12].
A partir de ce moment, le photographe fit beaucoup de conférences avec projection de diapositives et publia de nombreux articles dans des journaux et des revues. Pour financer son projet, il se livra à un travail de relations publiques d'une ampleur tout à fait inhabituelle pour un photographe. Ses apparitions dans la haute société révélèrent comme un charmant salonnard qui savait parler de tout et de rien. Il préférait cependant se présenter dans la panoplie de l'aventurier de l'Ouest sauvage, avec un chapeau mou à large bord. C'est dans cette tenue que le représente un autoportrait que le photographe a donné à imprimer dans toutes les publications possibles et imaginables et dont il fit bientôt réaliser un plus gros tirage en photogravure. Un contemporain décrit en ces termes l'aspect extérieur du photographe : «C'est un type amusant, à le voir comme ça […] il est grand et un peu anguleux. Il porte une mince cravate noire négligemment nouée, et il a toujours un chapeau dont on dirait que le tramway lui est passé dessus […] Les ondulations de sa voix lui donnent quelque chose de rêveur […] Il a des yeux bleus au regard ensommeillé avec au fond, une étincelle d'humour réprimée […] Il ne sourit jamais avec les lèvres. Les lèvres sont faites pour parler […] Il sait travailler et même se tuer à la tâche. Quand il travaille, il s'agite et remue tout autour de lui comme un cyclone. Il peut galoper plus vite que n'importe quel Indien et en cas de difficultés, il est encore plus endurant qu'eux[13].» Curtis

Lone Tree Lodge
Jicarilla, 1904

rough them."[13] Curtis became an established figure in public life, and his many activities increased his reputation, and yet the modest income that he earned as a photographer continued to be out of all proportion to his considerable costs.

In order to realize his organizational and publishing plans, in 1906 Curtis asked the railroad magnate and financier John Pierpont Morgan (1837–1913), whose acquaintance he had made through President Roosevelt, to back his project. Between 1898 and 1906 Curtis had drawn on his own limited means to fund his enterprise, and had already spent 25,000 dollars. He estimated that the work would require a further five years, and Morgan promised to cover the costs of the expeditions during this period to the tune of 15,000 dollars per annum. However, these 75,000 dollars were more of a bursary to which a number of strings were attached than a generous philanthropic donation. In return for his backing, Morgan received 300 original prints of Indian pictures, as well as 25 sets of the planned encyclopaedia. These he later donated to various scientific institutions of his choice. Morgan and Curtis agreed to sell *The North American Indian* on subscription at a price of 3,000 dollars for the complete 20-volume set. Individual volumes were not sold separately.

Each of the volumes adhered to the same basic concept, even if they sometimes varied in the details. They began with an alphabetical list of the phonetic symbols for the language of the tribes covered, followed by a register of the illustrations. In an introductory text Curtis presented the tribes in question and reported on his field work. As far as the contents were concerned, the texts on the individual Indian peoples were all constructed in a similar manner. As a rule, Curtis described the social and cultural life of a tribe in a specific region, giving the indi-

(1837–1913), den er über Roosevelt kennengelernt hatte, seine Unternehmung zu fördern. Zwischen 1898 und 1906 hatte Curtis sein Projekt mit begrenzten Mitteln selbst finanziert und bereits 25 000 Dollar ausgegeben. Er veranschlagte die weiteren Arbeiten auf fünf Jahre, und Morgan versprach, während dieser Zeit die Kosten für die Expeditionen in Höhe von 15 000 Dollar pro Jahr zu tragen. Diese 75 000 Dollar waren jedoch eher ein an zahlreiche Auflagen gebundenes Stipendium als eine großzügige Spende. Als Gegenleistung für seine Unterstützung erhielt Morgan 300 Originalabzüge von Indianerbildern sowie 25 Exemplare der geplanten Enzyklopädie, die er später an wissenschaftliche Institutionen seiner Wahl verschenkte. Morgan und Curtis beschlossen, das zwanzigbändige Werk *The North American Indian* als Subskription zu einem Gesamtpreis von 3000 Dollar zu vertreiben. Einzelbände konnten nicht erworben werden.

Inhaltlich folgt jeder Band einem grundlegenden, wenn auch nicht immer bis ins Detail durchgehaltenen Konzept: Zunächst wird eine alphabetische Liste der Lautschriftzeichen für die Sprache der vorgestellten indianischen Stämme präsentiert, anschließend folgt ein Verzeichnis der Illustrationen. Im einführenden Text stellt Curtis die Indianerstämme vor und berichtet von seinen Feldforschungen. Die Texte über die einzelnen indianischen Ethnien sind inhaltlich ähnlich aufgebaut. In der Regel beschreibt Curtis das gesellschaftlich-kulturelle Leben eines Stammes in einer bestimmten Region und gibt den einzelnen Abschnitten seines Textes Zwischenüberschriften wie: »Leben im Stammesgebiet«, »Sitten und Gebräuche« oder »Arbeit, Kunsthandwerk und Religion«. Die meisten Beschreibungen umfassen außerdem ein Kapitel zum Thema »Mythologie«, andere werden außerdem von einem Abschnitt »Medizin und Medizinmänner« oder »Zeremonien« abgerundet.

Da die nordamerikanischen Indianerstämme keine schriftlichen Zeugnisse besaßen, beschäftigte sich Curtis von Anfang an intensiv mit ihrer münd-

devint une personnalité de la vie publique et ses nombreuses activités accrurent encore son renom, pourtant les recettes escomptées par le photographe ne furent jamais à la hauteur des dépenses engagées.

Afin de pouvoir concrétiser ses plans sur le terrain et d'un point de vue éditorial, Curtis demanda en 1906 au financier et magnat des chemins de fer John Pierpont Morgan (1837–1913), dont il avait fait la connaissance par l'entremise de Roosevelt, de promouvoir son entreprise. Entre 1898 et 1906, il avait réussi à s'en sortir avec ses propres moyens, très limités, et avait déjà dépensé 25 000 dollars. Il évalua la durée des travaux à venir à cinq ans et Morgan lui promit de lui donner, pendant toute cette période, 15 000 dollars par an pour les expéditions. Mais l'attribution de ces 75 000 dollars ressemblait plutôt à celle d'une bourse sévèrement contrôlée qu'à un geste généreux. Morgan en contrepartie reçut 300 tirages originaux des photos d'Indiens ainsi que 25 séries de l'encyclopédie, qu'il offrit par la suite à des institutions scientifiques de son choix. Morgan et Curtis décidèrent d'un commun accord de vendre les 20 volumes de l'œuvre *The North American Indian* par souscription, au prix global de 3 000 dollars. Les volumes ne pouvaient pas être achetés séparément. Au niveau du contenu, chaque volume suit, même s'il ne le respecte pas toujours scrupuleusement, un même concept de base. Apparaît tout d'abord une liste alphabétique des signes phonétiques de la langue de la tribu dont il est question, immédiatement suivie par une table des illustrations. Dans le texte d'introduction, Curtis se livre à une présentation des tribus indiennes et fait le point sur les recherches qu'il a menées sur le terrain. Les textes sur les différentes tribus indiennes sont construits sur le même plan. Curtis fait une description de la vie sociale et culturelle d'une tribu originaire de telle ou telle région et donne aux différentes sections de son texte des sous-titres comme «La vie dans le territoire de la tribu», «Us et coutumes» ou encore «Travail, artisanat d'art et religion». La plupart des descriptions comportent

vidual sections of his text sub-headings such as "Life in the tribal region," "Customs and mores," or "Work, crafts and religion." Most of these descriptions also included a chapter on "Mythology," while others are additionally rounded off with a section "Medicine and medicine men" or "Ceremonies."

Since the North American Indian peoples had no written lore, Curtis directed his attention right from the start to their oral traditions. He noted down the biographies of prominent chieftains, warriors, medicine men and priests, wrote down the texts and music of the Indians' dances and songs, and even recorded the latter on wax cylinders which he later had transcribed into notes. Between 1895 and 1928, Curtis visited, as already mentioned, over eighty different Indian tribes, and essentially the order of the published volumes of his encyclopaedia corresponds with the chronology of his photographic expeditions and field research. Thus the photographer visited a broad range of different peoples, such as the Kwakiutl on the Pacific Coast, the Comanches, Apaches and Cree in their striking tipis on the wide open prairies and at the foot of the Rocky Mountains, and the Hopi and other Pueblo and adobe dwellers in the arid south-west. With his encyclopaedia, Curtis documented the whole spectrum of Indian cultures and ways of life. His work clearly reveals that our image of the mounted buffalo-hunting redskin is in no way representative of the North American Indian.

When the New World was discovered by Europeans in 1492, the American continent was populated by over 100 different Indian groups. Despite considerable differences between the individual tribes, nine cultural areas can be distinguished, corresponding to geographical regions: the Arctic, the subarctic, the north-west coast, California, the plateaus and Great Basin, the south-west, the Great Plains, the south-east, and the north-east. Cur-

lichen Überlieferung. Er zeichnete die Biographien der bedeutenden Häuptlinge, Krieger, Medizinmänner und Priester auf. Mit Hilfe eines frühen Edisonschen Wachswalzen-Aufnahmegeräts nahm er Musik auf, die er anschließend in Noten transkribierte. Zwischen 1895 und 1928 besuchte Curtis, wie erwähnt, über 80 verschiedene Indianerstämme, und die Reihenfolge der veröffentlichten Bände seiner Enzyklopädie entspricht im wesentlichen dem zeitlichen Ablauf seiner Photoexpeditionen und Feldforschungen. Der Photograph suchte so unterschiedliche indianische Völker auf wie die Kwakiutl an der Pazifikküste, die Comanchen, Apachen und Crees mit ihren markanten Tipis in den Weiten der Prärien und am Fuße der Rocky Mountains sowie die Hopi und andere Pueblo- und Adobe-Bewohner im regenarmen Südwesten. Mit seiner Enzyklopädie hat Curtis die Bandbreite an Kulturen und Lebensformen der Indianer dokumentiert. Sein Werk zeigt anschaulich, daß unser Bild des Büffel jagenden, reitenden Indianers in keiner Weise repräsentativ ist für den nordamerikanischen Indianer schlechthin.

Als die Europäer 1492 die Neue Welt entdeckten, lebten auf dem amerikanischen Kontinent mehrere hundert verschiedene indianische Gruppen. Obwohl zwischen den einzelnen Stämmen große Unterschiede bestehen, können entsprechend den geographischen Gegebenheiten neun Kulturareale unterschieden werden: die Arktis, die Subarktis, die Nordwestküste, Kalifornien, die Plateaus und Hochbecken, der Südwesten, die Plains, der Südosten und der Nordosten. Curtis hat alle diese Gebiete, von denen einige im folgenden kurz vorgestellt werden, besucht und dort die Indianer, die zu seiner Zeit bereits größtenteils in Reservaten lebten, photographiert.

Am nördlichen Rand des Kontinents lebten die Inuit, von ihren indianischen Nachbarn verächtlich Eskimos (Rohfleischesser) genannt. In der arktischen Welt ernährten sie sich primär von Fischen und Meeressäugern sowie einigen wenigen Landtieren, die bis in den fernen Norden vordrangen. An Land

en outre un chapitre « Mythologie », d'autres sont par ailleurs complétées par une section « Médecine et sorciers » ou « Cérémonies ».

Les tribus indiennes d'Amérique du Nord ne possédant pas de documents écrits, Curtis s'intéressa tout particulièrement, et ceci dès le début, à leurs traditions orales. Il mit par écrit les biographies des chefs, des guerriers, des sorciers et des prêtres importants. Grâce aux premiers cylindres de cire Edison, il enregistra leur musique qu'il transcrivit ensuite dans des partitions. C'est ainsi qu'entre 1895 et 1928, Curtis rendit visite à plus de 80 tribus, et la chronologie de la publication des volumes de son encyclopédie correspond dans l'ensemble à celle de ses expéditions photographiques et de ses recherches sur le terrain. Le photographe rendit visite à des populations indiennes aussi différentes que les Kwakiutl sur la côte du Pacifique, les Comanches, les Apaches et les Cree dans leurs tipis caractéristiques, dans les Grandes Prairies et au pied des Rocheuses, les Hopi, les Pueblos et autres habitants adobes du Sud-Ouest aride et poussiéreux. Curtis nous a livré avec son encyclopédie une documentation de l'éventail des cultures et des modes de vie des Indiens. Son œuvre montre très clairement que l'image que nous nous faisons de l'Indien à cheval ou en train de chasser le bison, n'est nullement représentative de « l'Indien d'Amérique du Nord ».

Quand les Européens découvrent le Nouveau Monde en 1492, plusieurs centaines d'ethnies indiennes différentes vivent sur le sous-continent américain. Bien qu'il existe des différences notoires entre les tribus, il est possible de distinguer en fonction des données géographiques neuf grandes aires culturelles : l'Arctique, la zone subarctique, la côte Nord-Ouest, la Californie, les Plateaux et les hauts bassins, le Sud-Ouest, les Grandes Plaines, le Sud-Est et le Nord-Est. Curtis a visité toutes ces régions, dont certaines font ci-après l'objet d'une brève présentation, et y a photographié les Indiens qui, déjà à son époque, vivaient pour la plupart dans des réserves.

tis visited all of these regions, some of which will shortly be looked at in more depth, and photographed the Indians, who by that time were already primarily to be found on the reservations.

Inhabiting the northern rim of the continent were the Inuits, who were given the disparaging name Eskimos ("raw meat eaters") by their Indian neighbours. Up there in the Arctic region, they subsisted primarily on fish and aquatic mammals, as well as on the few land animals that penetrated so far north. On land, the Inuits travelled by dog-sled, while at sea they hunted in kayaks and umiaks, wooden-framed boats stretched with sealskins. From the skins they also made their clothing.

To the south-east of the Inuits, in the subarctic, lived Athapascan- and Algonkin-speaking peoples, including the Cree and Chipewyan. The housing of the tribes in this region consisted of conical tipis loosely covered with animal hides or beech bark. The Indians of the subarctic hunted caribou in the tundra, red deer and elk in the deciduous forests, and also trapped rodents and other animals for their fur, which was sewn together to make clothes. Their snowshoes enabled them to traverse a countryside deep in snow.

In contrast to the subarctic, the climate of the North Pacific Coast was mild, and the region rich in natural food resources. The inhabitants had a great variety of fish and shellfish to feed on, not to mention roots and berries. This abundance allowed these Indians to devote a large amount of their time to social and religious activities. The tribes built permanent villages with houses made of cedar planks which bore the sign of the head clan and were flanked by totem poles. They developed a wide range of artistic forms of expression and spiritual ceremonies, which manifested the tribal hierarchy. During so-called *potlatches*,[14] to which guests from other villages

bewegten sich die Inuit auf Hundeschlitten fort. Zur Jagd auf dem Wasser benutzten sie Kajaks und Umiaka – Boote mit hölzernen Rahmen, über die Seehundfelle gespannt waren. Aus den Fellen stellten sie auch ihre Kleidung her. Südöstlich der Inuit lebten in der Subarktis die Athapaskisch und Algonquin sprechenden Völker, zu denen unter anderem die Cree und die Chipewyan gehören. Als Behausung dienten den Stämmen dieser Region konische Tipi, die mit losen Tierhäuten oder Birkenrinde bedeckt waren. In der Tundra jagten die Indianer der Subarktis Karibu, in den Laubwäldern Elche und Rotwild, und außerdem stellten sie Nage- und Pelztieren Fallen. Die Felle dieser Tiere wurden zu Kleidungsstücken verarbeitet. Schneeschuhe ermöglichten die Durchquerung der im Tiefschnee versunkenen Landschaft.

Im Gegensatz zur Subarktis war das Klima an der pazifischen Nordwestküste mild, und die Region war reich an Nahrungsressourcen. Eine Vielzahl von Fischsorten und Schalentieren, aber auch Wurzeln und Beeren ernährten die Bevölkerung. Dieser Reichtum ermöglichte es den Indianern, einen großen Teil ihrer Zeit dem sozialen und religiösen Leben zu widmen. Die Stämme errichteten feste Dörfer mit Häusern aus Zedernplanken, die das Zeichen der führenden Sippe trugen und von Totempfählen flankiert waren. Es entwickelten sich künstlerische Ausdruckformen und spirituelle Zeremonien, innerhalb derer sich die Stammeshierarchie manifestierte. Bei den *potlachs*[14], zu denen Gäste aus anderen Dörfern eingeladen wurden, bekräftigte die Führungsschicht des Ortes ihren Status dadurch, daß sie Nahrungsmittel, Kleidungsstücke und Gebrauchsgegenstände verschenkte.

Der semiaride Südwesten war von zahlreichen ethnischen Gruppen bevölkert, die sich zum Teil erheblich voneinander unterschieden. Die Hopi und andere Pueblo-Indianer lebten als Feldbauern in Städten aus Lehmbauten mit zahlreichen Terrassen. Um trotz der Trockenheit Landwirtschaft betreiben zu können, entwickelten sie ausgeklügelte Bewässerungssysteme und fingen

A l'extrémité Nord du continent vivaient les Inuit, que leurs voisins indiens appelaient de façon méprisante «esquimaux», c'est-à-dire mangeurs de viande crue. Ils se nourrissaient principalement de poissons et de mammifères marins, et aussi de quelques rares animaux sauvages qui parvenaient à s'aventurer jusque dans le grand Nord. Sur terre, les Inuit se déplaçaient dans des traîneaux. Sur l'eau, ils utilisaient pour chasser des kayaks et des umiaka, embarcations dont les cadres en bois étaient tendus de peaux de phoque. Ces peaux étaient également utilisées pour confectionner les vêtements.

Au Sud-Est des Inuit vivaient, dans les zones subarctiques, des populations parlant l'athapasquiche et l'algonquin, auxquelles appartenaient notamment les Cree et les Chipewyan. Les tribus de cette région avaient pour habitations des tipis en forme de cônes couverts de peaux d'animaux non fixées ou d'écorces de bouleaux. Les Indiens chassaient le caribou dans la toundra, l'élan, le cerf et le chevreuil dans les forêts de feuillus et posaient également des pièges à rongeurs et autres animaux à fourrure, laquelle était ensuite cousue pour faire des vêtements. Des chaussures adaptées leur permettaient par ailleurs de se frayer un chemin à travers la neige épaisse sous laquelle disparaissait le paysage.

A l'inverse des zones subarctiques, le climat de la côte Nord-Ouest du Pacifique était doux et la région riche en ressources naturelles. Une grande variété de poissons et de coquillages, mais aussi des baies et des racines pourvoyaient à l'alimentation de la population. Cette richesse permettait aux Indiens de consacrer une grande partie de leur temps à la vie religieuse et sociale. Les tribus érigeaient des villages «en dur» dont les maisons, construites avec des planches de cèdre, portaient le signe de la tribu dirigeante et étaient flanquées de totems faisant office de pilots. Cette région vit se déployer tout un éventail de formes d'expression artistique et de cérémonies religieuses au cours desquelles se manifestait la hiérarchie en vigueur dans la tribu. Les

were invited, the local leaders consolidated their status by making presents of food, garments and articles of daily use.

The semi-arid south-west was populated by numerous groups, which in part differed considerably from one another. The Hopi and other Pueblo Indians were farmers who lived in towns consisting of clay buildings with numerous terraces. The aridity of the land led them to develop ingenious irrigation systems and to catch every single drop of rain. Although the Pueblo Indians were among the first to be missionized by the Spanish, they often adhered to their ancient customs and rituals, and were organized in small theocracies. Other tribes of the south-west lived from hunting and gathering, and the hunters included a number of semi-nomadic groups.

The wide open grasslands of the plains form the central area of North America, the Midwest. The large herds of buffalo grazing there were easy prey for the Indians and provided their main source of sustenance. Their hides were tanned and the leather used for garments, containers and other items of daily use. Although the tribes originally lived more on the margins of the prairies, once they owned horses they forged their way as mounted nomads ever further into the central grasslands. The conflicts over territory and resources encouraged the emergence of a cult of warfare between the tribes.

Taken together with the conflicts between the Indians and white settlers, these intertribal feuds provided a welcome excuse for the government in Washington to mobilize its army for "pacificatory actions" and to resettle the Indians in remote reservations. If initial encounters between whites and Indians had been fairly amicable, from 1840 relations between them dramatically deteriorated, especially in the plains, as a result of the influx of white

jeden Regentropfen auf. Obwohl die Pueblo-Indianer schon früh von den Spaniern missioniert wurden, hielten sie häufig an ihren alten Gebräuchen und Ritualen fest und waren in kleinen Theokratien organisiert. Andere Stämme des Südwestens waren Sammler und Jäger, wobei zu letzteren auch halbnomadische Gruppen zählten.

Das ausgedehnte Grasland der Plains bildet mit seinen weiten Ebenen den zentralen Teil Nordamerikas, den mittleren Westen. Die dort grasenden großen Büffelherden waren leichte Beute für die Indianerstämme; die Tiere dienten ihnen als Hauptnahrungsmittel. Die Büffelhaut wurde gegerbt und das Leder zu Kleidungsstücken, Behältnissen und anderen Gegenständen des täglichen Bedarfs verarbeitet. Lebten die Stämme zunächst eher am Rand der Prärie, so drangen sie, seitdem sie Pferde besaßen, als berittene Nomaden immer weiter ins zentrale Grasland vor. Gebiets- und Ressourcenkonflikte begünstigten die Entstehung eines Kriegskults zwischen den Stämmen.

Neben den Konflikten mit den weißen Siedlern waren diese Fehden zwischen den Stämmen schließlich ein willkommener Anlaß für die Regierung in Washington, ihre Armee zu »Befriedungsaktionen« einzusetzen und die Indianer in entfernte Reservate umzusiedeln. Waren die ersten Begegnungen zwischen Indianern und Weißen zunächst relativ freundschaftlich verlaufen, so führten insbesondere in den Plains seit 1840 der Zustrom weißer Einwanderer und die Nachfrage nach Büffelfellen im Pelzgeschäft zu einer dramatischen Verschlechterung der Beziehungen zwischen den Weißen und den Indianer. Seit den 70er Jahren wurden systematisch drei Millionen Büffel abgeschlachtet, um den Indianern ihre Lebensgrundlage zu entziehen, was – so der zynische Kommentar des Bürgerkriegshelden Phillip Sheridan – Fortschritt und Zivilisation vorantrieb.

Unter der Führung des Dakota-Häuptlings Sitting Bull gelang es einem Bündnis mehrerer Indianerstämme 1876 zum letzten Mal, die Weißen zu be-

potlachs[14], auxquels étaient invités des habitants d'autres villages, étaient l'occasion pour la tribu dirigeante d'affirmer son statut en offrant victuailles, vêtements et objets d'usage courant. Le Sud-Ouest semi-aride était peuplé d'une multiplicité d'ethnies totalement différentes. Les Indiens Pueblo, vivaient dans des villes de torchis regorgeant de cultures en terrasses. L'aridité, qui leur faisait recueillir la moindre goutte de pluie, les avait conduits à développer d'ingénieux systèmes d'irrigation. Bien qu'évangélisés très tôt par les Espagnols, les Pueblos ont souvent conservé leurs coutumes et rituels, et leur organisation était celle de petites théocraties. D'autres tribus du Sud-Ouest vivaient de la cueillette et de la chasse. A cette dernière catégorie appartenaient également des groupes semi-nomades.

L'immense étendue des Grandes Plaines forme la partie centrale de l'Amérique du Nord, ce que l'on appelle le Middle West. Ses grands troupeaux de bisons étaient une proie facile pour les tribus, dont ils constituaient la nourriture principale. La peau de bison était tannée et le cuir utilisé pour la confection de vêtements, de récipients et autres objets de la vie quotidienne. Si à l'origine les tribus vivaient plutôt en bordure de la Prairie, elles devinrent nomades à partir du moment où elles eurent des chevaux et pénétrèrent de plus en plus loin à l'intérieur des Plaines. Des conflits de territoire et de ressources favorisèrent l'apparition d'un culte guerrier entre les tribus.

Pour le gouvernement de Washington, ces querelles entre les tribus furent finalement, en plus des conflits avec les colons blancs, une bonne occasion d'engager l'armée dans des «actions de pacification» et de déplacer les Indiens dans des réserves reculées. Si les premières rencontres entre Indiens et Blancs s'étaient passées de façon relativement amicale, l'afflux, surtout dans les Grandes Plaines, d'immigrés à partir de 1840 et la demande croissante de peaux de bison dans l'industrie de la fourrure débouchèrent sur une dégradation dramatique des relations entre Blancs et Indiens. A partir des

The Apache
Der Apache
L'Apache
1906

settlers and the demand for buffalo hides for commercial purposes. From the 1870s onwards, three million buffaloes were systematically slaughtered in order to deprive the Indians of the basis of their existence. This, as the hero of the Civil Wars, General Phillip Sheridan, cynically remarked, advanced progress and civilization.

Under the leadership of the Dakota chieftain Sitting Bull, an alliance of several Indian tribes managed in 1876 to defeat the whites for the last time. The Battle of Little Bighorn River cost General George Armstrong Custer and 200 of his soldiers their lives. But this was to be Indians' last major victory. A year later Chief Joseph and his Nez Percé were forced to abandon their struggle and were deported to the southern prairies. The ousting of the Indians from their ancestral territories culminated in 1890 in the Battle of Wounded Knee.

During his research expeditions, Edward Curtis also devoted much attention to these wars. He had the site of the Battle of Little Bighorn shown to him and interviewed eyewitnesses. The Battle of Wounded Knee, in which US troops indiscriminately killed women and children, was described by Curtis as a massacre. He wanted to make a record of the event, as seen from the Indians' point of view, and to this end wrote down their orally transmitted war reports fifty years after the battle took place.

The last volume of Curtis' encyclopaedia is devoted to the Inuits of the Bering Strait. In it, the now 59-year-old photographer noted with regret that poor health had prevented him from spending the winter in the extreme north, and thus from photographing igloos and other snow shelters. Content nevertheless with the result of his work, he concluded the last volume of his opus with the words: "Great is the satisfaction the writer enjoys when he can at least say to all those whose faith has been unbounded, 'It is finished.'" [15]

siegen. Die Schlacht am Little Bighorn River kostete General George Armstrong Custer und 200 Soldaten das Leben. Doch dies sollte der letzte große Sieg der Indianer sein. Schon ein Jahr später wurden Chief Joseph und seine Nez Percé zur Aufgabe ihres Kampfes gezwungen und in die südliche Prärie deportiert. Die Verdrängung der Indianer aus ihren angestammten Gebieten endete 1890 mit der Schlacht von Wounded Knee.

Edward Curtis hat sich während seiner Forschungsreisen auch mit diesen Kriegen auseinandergesetzt. Er ließ sich den Ort zeigen, an dem die Schlacht am Little Bighorn stattgefunden hatte und interviewte Augenzeugen. Als Massaker bezeichnete Curtis die Schlacht von Wounded Knee, in der die US-Truppen wahllos Frauen und Kinder getötet hatten. Um die Sicht der Indianer auf dieses Ereignis zu bewahren, schrieb er 50 Jahre später ihre nur mündlich überlieferten Kriegsberichte nieder.

Der letzte Band der Enzyklopädie ist den Inuit der Beringstraße gewidmet. Der inzwischen 59jährige Photograph stellt darin bedauernd fest, daß er wegen seiner angeschlagenen Gesundheit den Winter nicht im hohen Norden verbringen und daher auch keine Iglus und andere Schneebehausungen photographieren konnte. Gleichwohl glücklich mit dem Ergebnis seiner Arbeit, schließt er den letzten Band seines Opus mit den Worten: »Groß ist die Befriedigung des Autors, wenn er all jenen, die an ihn geglaubt haben, sagen kann: ›Es ist vollendet.‹« [15]

Während seines gesamten Schaffens hat Curtis seine Photos auf sehr unterschiedlichen Materialien abgezogen. Ausschlaggebend für die Wahl des Materials war der Verwendungszweck der Reproduktionen. Ältere Prints sind noch auf Albuminpapier hergestellt worden. Im Feld stellte er von seinen frisch entwickelten Negativen zunächst die leicht herzustellenden Cyanotypie-Kontaktabzüge als Arbeitskopien her. Für Ausstellungsvergrößerungen wählte er oft Papiere mit matter oder rauher Oberfläche. [16] Curtis experimen-

années 70, trois millions de bisons furent systématiquement abattus, privant ainsi les Indiens de leurs ressources vitales, afin que puisse se poursuivre ce que le cynique commentaire du général Phillip Sheridan, héros de la guerre civile, appelait « le progrès de la civilisation ».

Sous la conduite du chef indien du Dakota Sitting Bull, plusieurs tribus réunies avaient réussi pour la dernière fois à vaincre les Blancs en 1876. La bataille de Little Bighorn avait coûté la vie au général George Armstrong Custer et à 200 soldats. Mais cette grande victoire des Indiens devait être la dernière. Un an plus tard, le chef indien Joseph et ses Nez Percé étaient contraints d'abandonner leur combat et déportés dans le sud de la Prairie. L'éviction des Indiens de leurs territoires ancestraux s'acheva en 1890 avec la bataille de Wounded Knee. Edward Curtis s'est également intéressé à ces guerres durant ses expéditions. Il se fit montrer l'endroit où avait eu lieu la bataille de Little Bighorn et interviewa des témoins oculaires. Il qualifia de carnage la bataille de Wounded Knee au cours de laquelle les troupes américaines avaient à l'aveuglette massacré femmes et enfants en 1890. Curtis, qui voulait que cet événement fût consigné du point de vue des Indiens, mit donc par écrit, 50 années plus tard, les récits qu'ils lui avaient faits de la guerre et qui jusque-là n'avaient été transmis que par voie orale.

Dans le dernier volume, consacré aux Inuit du détroit de Béring, le photographe, alors âgé de 59 ans, constate avec regret que sa santé défaillante ne lui a pas permis de passer l'hiver dans le grand Nord et par conséquent de photographier les igloos et autres habitations en blocs de neige. Ce qui ne l'empêche pas de mettre avec contentement un point final à son œuvre, dont le dernier volume s'achève sur ces lignes : « Grande est la satisfaction de l'auteur quand il peut dire à tous ceux qui ont cru en lui : C'est fini [15]. »

Pendant toute la durée de sa production, Curtis a tiré ses photographies sur des supports très diversifiés, choisis en fonction de la destination des repro-

Throughout his entire creative life, Curtis printed his photos onto very many different materials. Decisive for the choice of material was the use to which the reproduction would be put. Older prints were still made on albumenized paper. When working in the field, he initially made from his freshly developed negatives easily produced cyanotype contact prints as his working copies. Enlargements for exhibitions were often done on matt or rough-textured paper.[16] Curtis experimented with a variety of techniques, such as silver-free platinum and palladium prints, and other mixed forms that have yet to receive closer study.

However, Curtis reproduced most of his negatives as silver gelatin prints. On these prints, the image surface shows the negative number and copyright sign, to which the photographer attached great importance. With regard to the dating, it should be noted that the year given beneath his photographs always refers to the date of the copyright and not of the actual exposure.[17] It was silver gelatin prints that as a rule Curtis submitted to the Library of Congress in order to register his copyright, with the result that the Copyright Deposit in Washington has ended up with the most extensive collection of vintage Curtis prints. Silver gelatin prints were also used as the originals for the numerous newspaper and magazine articles on his project, as well as for the encyclopaedia itself.

For *The North American Indian* Curtis had his photographic work reproduced by the best technology of the day: photogravure. This intaglio process, which involves virtually no screening and no silver – meaning that it remains by and large immutable – permitted the originals to be individually finished by highly qualified retouchers and printers.[18]

tierte mit verschiedenen Verfahren wie den silberfreien Platin- und Palladium-abzügen und weiteren, bisher nicht näher erforschten Mischformen.

Die meisten seiner Werke reproduzierte Curtis jedoch als Silbergelatine-Prints. Auf diesen Abzügen sind in der Bildfläche die Negativnummer und der Copyrightvermerk lesbar, auf die der Photograph großen Wert legte. Bei der Frage der Datierung ist zu beachten, daß die unter den Photographien angegebenen Jahreszahlen sich stets auf das Datum des Copyrights und nicht auf das Datum der Aufnahme beziehen.[17] Mit Silbergelatine-Abzügen meldete Curtis in der Regel bei der Library of Congress das Copyright für seine Photos an. Aufgrund der zahlreichen Belegphotos, die Curtis an die Bibliothek schickte, ist das Copyright-Deposit in Washington die umfangreichste Sammlung von Curtis' Vintage prints. Silbergelatine-Prints dienten auch als Druckvorlagen für die zahlreichen Publikationen über sein Projekt in Zeitungen und Zeitschriften sowie für die Enzyklopädie selbst.

In *The North American Indian* ließ Curtis sein photographisches Werk in der besten Technik reproduzieren, die seinerzeit zur Verfügung stand: der Photogravüre. Dieses praktisch rasterlose, silberfreie und damit weitgehend unveränderliche Tiefdruckverfahren ließ eine individuelle Bearbeitung der Photovorlagen durch hochqualifizierte Retuscheure und Drucker zu.[18]

Curtis' Indianerphotographien wurden über sein Atelier auch außerhalb des *North American Indian*-Projekts angeboten und kosteten je nach Größe zwischen 3 und 20 Dollar.[19] Das Studio verkaufte außerdem besonders edle und aufwendige, oft großformatige Abzüge. Sie waren als Wandschmuck gedacht; schwere Holzrahmen wurden gleich mitgeliefert. In dieser Präsentationsform folgen sie den Konventionen der piktoralistischen Kunstphotographie der Zeit. Diese neigte zur impressionistischen Bildatmosphäre und strebte statt photographischer Schärfe weiche Bildtöne an. Im Bildaufbau beschränkt sich der Piktoralismus häufig auf ein wesentliches Motiv, das vor weitgehend

ductions. Les épreuves les plus anciennes étaient encore réalisées sur du papier albuminé. Celles qu'il réalisait sur le terrain à partir des négatifs qu'il venait de développer étaient des cyanotypes facilement manipulables, obtenus par contact et qui lui servaient d'abord d'épreuves de travail. Les agrandissements qui devaient être exposés étaient souvent tirés sur des papiers mats ou durs[16]. Curtis expérimenta différents procédés comme le tirage au platine ou au palladium, exempts de sels d'argent, ainsi que d'autres combinaisons sur lesquelles on ne s'était guère penché jusqu'alors.

Mais dans l'ensemble, Curtis tirait ses œuvres sous la forme d'épreuves gélatino-argentiques. On peut lire sur ces clichés, au recto de la photographie, le numéro du négatif et la mention de copyright, auxquels le photographe tenait beaucoup. Soulignons en ce qui concerne la datation que l'année qui figure sur ses photos se rapporte toujours à la date du copyright, et non à celle de la prise de vue[17].

Ce sont en général des épreuves gélatino-argentiques que déposait Curtis à la Library of Congress pour les besoins du copyright. Par le grand nombre de photos qu'il a envoyées, à titre de justificatifs, à cette bibliothèque, le bureau du copyright de Washington représente la plus importante collection de vintages de Curtis. Ce sont également des épreuves gélatino-argentiques qui servaient de copies pour les nombreuses publications de son projet dans des journaux et des revues, ainsi que pour l'encyclopédie elle-même.

Dans les *North American Indian*, Curtis fit reproduire son œuvre photographique au moyen de la technique la plus perfectionnée dont on disposât à cette époque, à savoir la photogravure. Ce procédé d'héliogravure pratiquement sans trame, exempt de toute substance argentique et par conséquent en grande partie inaltérable, permettait un traitement individuel des épreuves par des retoucheurs et des imprimeurs hautement qualifiés[18].

En dehors du projet des *North American Indian*, les photos d'Indiens de

Curtis' Indian photographs were also available for purchase from his studio, separate from the *North American Indian* project, and cost between 3 and 20 dollars, depending on their size. [19] In addition to these, the studio also sold particularly fine and lavishly made prints, often in large formats and complete with heavy wooden frames, which were destined to adorn parlour walls. Presented in this form, they were in keeping with the contemporary conventions of pictorialist art photography. This tended towards an impressionistic atmosphere in which photographic sharpness gave way to soft tones. Compositionally, pictorialism often restricted itself to one basic motif presented before a largely neutral background. Curtis also made use of such compositional elements, but in terms of subject matter his pictures differ radically from pictorialist photographs.

One of Curtis' specialities were "Curt-tònes" [sic], also known as orotones or goldtones, photographs printed on glass plates with a gold-tinted background, meant to be hung in a frame. As an advertisement from his studio put it: "The new Curt-tone finish of the Indian studies is most unusual in its depth and lifelike brilliancy. Of this remarkable finish Mr Curtis says: 'The ordinary photographic print lacks depth … and transparency, or more strictly speaking, translucency. We all know how beautiful are the stones and pebbles in the limpid brook of the forest where the water absorbs the blue of the sky and the green of the foliage, yet when we take the same iridescent pebbles from the water and dry them they are dull and lifeless, so it is with the orthodox photographic print, but in the Curt-tones all the translucency is retained and they are as full of life and sparkle as an opal." [20] With the introduction of the orotones, the Indian photographs became socially acceptable wall decoration, and the Curtis Studio was able to supply a wide clientele with photographic reproductions in the most diverse qualities.

neutralem Hintergrund wiedergegeben wird. Auch Curtis hat diese Gestaltungselemente eingesetzt, jedoch unterscheiden sich seine Aufnahmen vom Sujet her grundlegend von den piktorialistischen Bildern.
Eine Curtis-Spezialität waren »Curt-tònes« [sic], auch als Orotones oder Goldtones bekannt, eine Art von Hinterglasbildern mit goldgefärbtem Hintergrund zur Präsentation im Wandrahmen. In einer Werbung des Studios heißt es: »Die neuen Curt-tònes der indianischen Studien sind in ihrer Tiefe und Lebensechtheit höchst ungewöhnlich. Über diese bemerkenswerte Ausführung sagt Mr. Curtis: ›Dem gewöhnlichen photographischen Abzug mangelt es an Tiefe und Durchsichtigkeit oder, genauer gesprochen, an Durchscheinbarkeit. Wir alle wissen, wie schön das Gestein und die Kiesel auf dem Grund eines rauschenden Baches im Wald aussehen, wenn das Wasser das Blau des Himmels und das Grün der Blätter aufnimmt. Doch wenn wir denselben leuchtenden Kiesel aus dem Wasser nehmen und trocknen, dann ist er stumpf und leblos. So verhält es sich auch mit den herkömmlichen photographischen Abzügen, doch in den Curt-tònes wird das durchscheinende Element erhalten: Die Bilder leben und funkeln wie Opale. Die Curt-tònes werden mit einem besonderen, für sie speziell gefertigten schönen Rahmen in verschiedenen Größen geliefert.«[20] Mit den Orotones wurden die Indianerphotographien als Wandschmuck salonfähig, und das Curtis-Studio konnte mit den Photoreproduktionen unterschiedlichster Qualität eine breite Käuferschicht bedienen.
Selbstverständlich hatte es bereits lange vor Curtis Abbildungen von Indianern gegeben. »Die amerikanische Ethnologie beginnt mit Catlin«, heißt es bei Michael Mooney. [21] George Catlins (1796–1872) Waffen im Kampf gegen das Vergessen waren Bleistift und Pinsel. »Um das äußere Erscheinungsbild und die Sitten der untergehenden Stämme der nordamerikanischen Ureinwohner vor dem Vergessen zu bewahren«[22], malte, skizzierte und beschrieb

Curtis connurent un autre débouché commercial via son atelier, où elles coûtaient entre trois et vingt dollars selon le format[19]. Le studio vendait par ailleurs des épreuves particulièrement luxueuses et coûteuses. Les tirages, souvent en grand format, étaient pensés comme des décorations murales et livrés, à l'instar de celles-ci, avec de lourds cadres de bois. Cette présentation ne faisait en réalité que suivre les conventions de la photographie pictorialiste de l'époque, qui cherchait à créer une atmosphère impressionniste et privilégiait la douceur du chromatisme au détriment de la netteté photographique. Par la construction de l'image, le pictorialisme se limite souvent à un motif principal qui se détache sur un fond en grande partie neutre. Si Curtis a lui aussi intégré ces éléments de composition, ses clichés se distinguent néanmoins, de par le sujet, des images pictorialistes.
Une des spécialités de Curtis étaient les « Curt-tònes » [sic], connus également sous le nom de « tons or », sortes de photos à fonds dorés, sous verre, et destinées à figurer dans un cadre. Dans une publicité de l'atelier, on peut lire : « Les nouveaux tons or des études d'Indiens sont tout à fait exceptionnels du point de vue de leur profondeur et du rendu fidèle qu'ils donnent de la vie. Ecoutons Mr. Curtis parler de cette réalisation remarquable : ‹L'épreuve photographique habituelle manque de profondeur et de transparence, ou plus exactement de la sensation de transparence. Nous savons tous à quel point le fond d'un ruisseau qui murmure dans une forêt, avec l'eau qui absorbe le bleu du ciel et le vert des feuilles, exalte la beauté des roches et des cailloux. Mais qu'on retire de l'eau ce même caillou tout brillant et qu'on le sèche, et il se retrouve terne et sans vie. Il en va de même des tirages photographiques traditionnels, mais les Curt-tònes ont en eux cet élément de transparence grâce auquel les images vivent et scintillent comme des opales. Ils sont livrés avec un beau cadre spécialement conçu pour eux, dans différents formats[20]. » Nimbées de tons dorés, les photographies d'Indiens

Pictures of Indians had already been around long before Curtis took an interest in them. "American anthropology begins with Catlin", writes Michael Mooney.[21] The weapons George Catlin (1796–1872) used in the struggle to prevent ethnic peoples from being forgotten were the pen and the brush. He painted, sketched and described everything he saw in order to save "from oblivion the looks and customs of the vanishing races of native men in America."[22] In 1841 this adventurer, painter and reporter published the documentation he had amassed between 1832 and 1836 as *Letters and Notes on the North American Indian.*

Catlin was the first person to recommend, even if to no avail, the setting up of national parks so as to keep intact at least a few territories of the West. His proposal to establish an Indian museum was turned down in the US Senate by a majority of just one vote, despite the important advocacy of Daniel Webster. Much as Curtis was to do later, Catlin expressed the personal need to document everything before it was irretrievably lost. In some cases his records are the last to bear witness to the culture and history of a tribe before it was wiped out, for example by the fatal chicken pox epidemic that raged in 1837. If there was one person whose work set an example to Curtis, it was certainly Catlin.

In the field of photography, too, Curtis had a number of forerunners. He was by no means the first to photograph Indians. The itinerant daguerreotypists who had followed the pioneers' treks had known how to lure the Indians before their cameras with their promises. Early on, pictures of "savages adorned with feathers" were to be seen in display cases in small towns, and at the latest since the Civil Wars almost every American small town had its photographers or was at least visited by travelling photographers passing through.

er alles, was er sah. 1841 veröffentlichte der Abenteurer, Maler und Reporter seine zwischen 1832 und 1836 entstandene Dokumentation *Letters and Notes on the North American Indian.*

Catlin empfahl als erster – wenn auch vergebens – die Einrichtung von Nationalparks, um wenigstens einige Gebiete des Westens in ihrer Ursprünglichkeit zu bewahren. Seinen Vorschlag, ein Indianermuseum einzurichten, lehnte der US-Senat trotz der prominenten Fürsprache von Daniel Webster mit nur einer Stimme Mehrheit ab. Ähnlich wie später Curtis äußerte bereits Catlin, er fühle sich verpflichtet, alles zu dokumentieren, bevor es unwiederbringlich verloren sei. In einigen Fällen sind seine Aufzeichnungen die letzten, die Zeugnis von der Kultur und der Geschichte eines Stammes ablegen, bevor dieser ausgelöscht wurde, etwa durch die 1837 wütende, tödliche Windpockenepidemie. Wenn es eine Person gibt, an deren Wirken sich Curtis ein Beispiel genommen hat, war dies mit Sicherheit Catlin.

Auch auf dem Gebiet der Photographie hatte Curtis Vorläufer. Er war keinesfalls der erste, der Indianer aufnahm. Bereits die Wander-Daguerreotypisten, die den Siedlertrecks gefolgt waren, hatten es verstanden, die Indianer gegen Versprechungen vor die Kamera zu locken. Aufnahmen »federgeschmückter Wilder« hingen schon früh in den Schaukästen kleiner Städte, und spätestens seit dem Bürgerkrieg besaß beinahe jede amerikanische Kleinstadt ihren Photographen oder wurde zumindest von durchreisenden Lichtbildnern besucht. Die Photographen waren ausnahmslos Weiße, und ihre Aufnahmen manifestierten den »weißen Blick« auf die indianische Population, die dem Bild, das von ihr fabriziert wurde, nichts entgegensetzen konnte. Auf den ersten Blick ergeben die Indianerphotographien ein uneinheitliches und widersprüchliches Bild: Repräsentiert werden sowohl der stolze Häuptling als auch der primitive, der kindliche und der wilde Indianer. Diese stereotypen Bilder reflektieren die ambivalente und wechselhafte Einstellung der weißen ameri-

pouvaient alors entrer dans les salons comme décorations murales, et le Studio Curtis toucher une vaste clientèle en proposant des reproductions de qualité tout à fait inégale.

Bien entendu, on avait déjà représenté des Indiens bien avant Curtis. «L'ethnologie américaine commence avec Catlin» – c'est du moins ce qu'écrit Michael Mooney.[21] Le crayon et le pinceau étaient ses armes dans le combat qu'il menait contre l'oubli. George Catlin (1796–1872) peignait, faisait des croquis et décrivait tout ce qu'il voyait «pour sauver de l'oubli l'aspect extérieur et les coutumes des premiers habitants de l'Amérique du Nord et de leurs tribus en voie d'extinction[22]». Cet aventurier, peintre et reporter publia en 1841 la documentation qu'il avait rassemblée entre 1832 et 1836 sous le titre *Letters and Notes on the North American Indian.*

Même si ses conseils ne furent pas suivis d'effets, Catlin fut le premier à recommander, en ce qui concernait l'aménagement de parcs nationaux, que soit conservé, du moins pour quelques territoires de l'Ouest, leur agencement d'origine. En dépit du poids de l'intervention de Daniel Webster, le sénat américain rejeta, à une voix seulement, son projet de création d'un musée indien. Comme Curtis plus tard, Catlin exprimait déjà le sentiment qu'il était nécessaire de tout documenter avant que les choses soient irrémédiablement perdues. Ses dessins et ses notes sont parfois les derniers témoignages que nous ayons sur la culture et l'histoire d'une tribu juste avant qu'elle disparaisse, par exemple à cause de la terrible et mortelle épidémie de varicelle de 1837. S'il y a une personne dont l'action a servi de modèle à Curtis, c'est bien certainement Catlin.

En photographie également, Curtis, qui n'était nullement le premier à faire des clichés des Indiens, avait des précurseurs. Les daguerréotypistes ambulants qui avaient suivi les convois des colons avaient appris à attirer les Indiens devant leur appareil en échange de promesses. Très tôt déjà on put

The photographers were without exception white, and their pictures revealed the "white view" of the Indian population, which could do nothing to counter the image created of it. At first sight the Indian photographs present an inconsistent and contradictory picture, showing as they do not only the proud chieftain, but also the primitive, the childlike, and the savage Indian. These stereotype images reflect the white American populace's ambivalent and shifting view of the Indians. Initially, during the second half of the 19th century, they were seen as mortal foes, after the turn of the century they were stylized as "noble savages," and during the Great Depression they virtually disappeared from peoples' minds.

Three different groups of photographers took Indians as their motif. The official geological government expeditions were accompanied by photographers who took pictures of impressive landscapes, such as the Grand Cañon or the sinter terraces of the Yellowstone region, but who also photographed their Indian scouts. This was mostly done in the popular stereograph format, which was especially suited to taking snapshots of people – and which was most readily saleable once the expedition was over. The second group, the studio photographers of the East Coast, enticed the Indian delegations that travelled to negotiations in Washington onto their premises, and then sold the pictures of the "diplomats in buckskin" as curiosities. The third and largest group comprised the hosts of photographers who had opened small studios in the new provincial settlements in the West, and who photographed anything that brought them money. Their Indian photographs satisfied the small-town inhabitants' demands for pictures of the strange savages, and consequently reflected the population's prejudices towards the Indians. Curtis' dealings with the Indians were also not always uncontroversial, and yet he was far

kanischen Bevölkerung gegenüber den Indianern. In der zweiten Hälfte des 19. Jahrhunderts galten sie zunächst als Todfeinde, nach der Jahrhundertwende wurden sie zu »edlen Wilden« stilisiert, und in der Zeit der Weltwirtschaftskrise nahm man sie kaum noch zur Kenntnis.

Drei verschiedene Gruppen von Photographen wählten die Indianer als Bildmotiv. Die offiziellen geologischen Regierungsexpeditionen wurden von Photographen begleitet, die Aufnahmen von der beeindruckenden Landschaft wie dem Grand Canyon oder den Sinterterrassen des Yellowstone-Gebiets machten. Außerdem photographierten sie ihre indianischen Begleiter, die Scouts. Meist geschah dies im populären Stereoformat, das für Schnappschüsse von Menschen besonders geeignet war – und sich nach Abschluß der Reise auch am besten verkaufen ließ. Die Atelierphotographen der Ostküste lockten die Indianerdelegationen, die zu Verhandlungen nach Washington reisten, in ihre Studios und verkauften die Bilder der »Diplomaten in Büffelleder« anschließend als Kuriosität. Die dritte und größte Gruppe waren die zahlreichen Photographen, die in den neuen kleinstädtischen Siedlungen des Westens ein Atelier eröffnet hatten und alles photographierten, womit Geld zu verdienen war. Mit ihren Indianeraufnahmen befriedigten sie die Nachfrage der Kleinstadtbevölkerung und der Reisenden nach Bildern von den fremden Wilden, bestätigten mit ihren Photos aber auch die in der Bevölkerung vorhandenen Vorurteile gegenüber den Indianern.

Auch Curtis' Umgang mit den Indianern war nicht immer unumstritten, doch den meisten seiner Zeitgenossen war er weit voraus. Es erfüllte ihn mit Zorn, wenn sich die schon fast zur Tradition gewordenen Ungerechtigkeiten der Weißen gegenüber den Indianern in seinen Tagen fortsetzten.

1914 drehte Curtis unter dem Titel *Im Land der Kopfjäger* einen Spielfilm über das Leben der Indianer an der Nordwestküste. Curtis inszenierte diesen kolorierten Stummfilm, dessen Handlung auf Legenden und mündlichen Überlie-

voir des photos de «sauvages en parures de plumes» dans les vitrines des petites villes, et au moins depuis la guerre, chaque petite ville américaine avait son photographe ou du moins recevait la visite de photographes ambulants. Les photographes étaient sans exception blancs et leurs clichés reflétaient le regard des Blancs sur la population indienne, qui elle-même se trouvait démunie face à l'image qu'on fabriquait d'elle. Ce qui au premier coup d'œil ressort de ces photographies, c'est l'image hétérogène et contradictoire qu'elles donnent des Indiens. On y représente aussi bien le chef dans toute sa fierté que l'Indien primitif, sauvage et proche de l'enfant. Ces photos stéréotypées réfléchissaient l'ambivalence et l'instabilité de l'attitude de la population américaine envers les Indiens. Considérés comme des ennemis mortels dans la seconde moitié du XIXe siècle, puis idéalisés de façon tout aussi réductrice comme des «êtres nobles et farouches», c'est à peine si on avait encore vent de leur existence à l'époque de la crise économique mondiale.

Les photographes dont le sujet était les Indiens se répartissaient en trois groupes. Les expéditions géologiques ministérielles étaient accompagnées par des photographes officiels qui prenaient des clichés du paysage grandiose comme le Grand Canyon ou les terrasses de concrétions du parc de Yellowstone, et photographiaient également leurs accompagnateurs indiens. Ils utilisaient le plus souvent le format stéréoscopique alors très populaire, celui qui se prêtait le mieux aux instantanés de personnes … et qui, le voyage terminé, se vendait au prix le plus avantageux. Les photographes de studio de la côte Est attiraient dans leurs ateliers les délégations indiennes venues à Washington en pourparlers, à la suite de quoi ils vendaient comme des curiosités les photos des «diplomates en peaux de bison». Le troisième groupe, le plus important, était celui des nombreux photographes qui avaient ouvert un petit atelier dans les nouveaux lotissements des petites villes de l'Ouest et photographiaient tout ce qui pouvait leur rapporter de l'argent. En photo-

ahead of most of his contemporaries. It filled him with rage that the injustices of the whites towards the Indians continued in his day, injustices that had almost become rooted as a tradition.

In 1914 Curtis shot *In the Land of the Headhunters*, a feature film, subsequently hand-coloured, on the life of the Indians of the north-west coast. The plot was based on Indian lore and legends, and Curtis staged this silent movie in a non-realistic manner adding a touch of violence and sentimental romanticism, all quite in keeping with the film medium. He dressed the Indians according to his own conceptions, and took stills during the shooting which he later included in his books, albeit without designating them as set photos – for which he was understandably reproached by scientists in the years thereafter.

The fact that an Indian ethnic group was placed at the centre of the film and determined the entire plot made Curtis' work a first in film history. The film was shown several times in Seattle, and once again Curtis brought his excellent connections with the local press into play, which wrote: "In the face of almost insurmountable difficulties [he] has now made himself a leading authority. A new term has indeed been created for him, 'photo-historian'."[23] The film failed to be a great public success, but it left its mark on younger film-makers with an ethnographic leaning, such as Robert Flaherty (1884–1951), who rose to fame with his classic Inuit film *Nanook of the North* (1922).

It is only very recently that Curtis has met with greater interest as an author and researcher of Indians. For years his exceptional and comprehensive life's work remained underappreciated. Even Curtis' contemporaries reacted in markedly different ways to his undertaking. Despite Roosevelt's political backing, his project found no

ferungen beruhte, wirklichkeitsfern und filmgerecht angereichert mit einer Prise Gewalt und sentimentaler Romantik. Er kostümierte die Indianer nach seinen Vorstellungen und nahm bei den Dreharbeiten Standbilder auf, die später in seinen Büchern auftauchten, ohne als Filmstills gekennzeichnet zu sein – was ihm die Wissenschaftler in der Folgezeit verständlicherweise vorwarfen. Die Tatsache, daß eine indianische Ethnie im Mittelpunkt des Filmes steht und das gesamte dramatische Geschehen bestimmt, machte Curtis' Werk filmgeschichtlich zu einem Novum. In Seattle wurde der Film mehrfach aufgeführt, wobei Curtis wieder seine guten Beziehungen zur örtlichen Presse spielen ließ, die schrieb: »Im Angesicht fast unüberwindlicher Schwierigkeiten hat er sich nun zur führenden Autorität der indianischen Stämme daheim und in der Wildnis erhoben. Tatsächlich ist ein neuer Ausdruck für ihn entworfen worden: der eines ›Photo-Historikers‹.«[23] Dem Film war kein großer Publikumserfolg beschieden, aber er prägte jüngere, ethnographisch arbeitende Filmemacher wie zum Beispiel Robert Flaherty (1884–1951), der mit seinem Inuit-Spielfilm *Nanuk, der Eskimo* (1922) zu Ruhm gelangte.

Als Autor und »Indianerforscher« findet Curtis erst in jüngster Zeit stärkere Beachtung. Jahrelang wurde sein außergewöhnliches und umfangreiches Lebenswerk nicht angemessen gewürdigt. Bereits Curtis' Zeitgenossen reagierten sehr unterschiedlich auf das Projekt. Trotz Roosevelts politischer Unterstützung wurde es staatlicherseits nicht gefördert, weder von der Smithsonian Institution noch vom American Bureau of Ethnology. Den etablierten Ethnologen und Anthropologen war Curtis' Tätigkeit suspekt. Der Photograph konnte keine akademische Ausbildung vorweisen, war aber aufgrund seiner Kontakte zu hochgestellten Persönlichkeiten und dank seiner Vortragskünste bekannter als mancher Professor. Die Wissenschaftler nahmen vor allem Anstoß am Kunstcharakter der Photographie. Curtis wollte die Ergebnisse seiner Forschungsreisen in künstlerischer Form präsentieren.

graphiant les Indiens, ils satisfaisaient la demande d'images de sauvages allogènes de la population des petites villes et des voyageurs, et confirmaient leurs préjugés à l'égard des Indiens. L'attitude de Curtis envers les Indiens fut, elle aussi, parfois controversée ; il faut néanmoins souligner qu'il était très en avance sur la plupart de ses contemporains. Il entrait dans des colères noires quand il voyait, ce qui était presque devenu une tradition, les Blancs continuer de perpétrer, à son époque, des injustices envers les Indiens.

En 1914, Curtis tourna un film colorié ultérieurement sur la vie des Indiens de la côte Nord-Ouest intitulé *Au pays des chasseurs de têtes*, et dont l'action reposait sur des légendes et des transmissions orales. La mise en scène de ce film muet était très éloignée de la réalité et en même temps très « cinématographique », dans le sens où elle était agrémentée d'une pincée de violence et de sentimentalisme romantique. Les Indiens portaient des costumes que lui-même avait imaginés et pendant les séances de tournage, il prenait des photographies qu'il intégra plus tard dans ses livres mais sans les identifier en tant que photogrammes, ce qui, on peut le comprendre, lui valut l'opprobre des scientifiques.

Le fait qu'une ethnie indienne soit au centre du film et conditionne toute l'intrigue faisait de l'œuvre de Curtis quelque chose de tout à fait nouveau dans l'histoire du cinéma. A Seattle, le film fut projeté à plusieurs reprises et une fois de plus, Curtis fit jouer ses relations dans la presse locale, laquelle écrivait : « Confronté à des difficultés presque insurmontables, il a su se hausser jusqu'à devenir une autorité majeure en matière de tribus indiennes, que ce soient celles de la région ou celles de contrées sauvages. En réalité, on a conçu pour lui une nouvelle expression, celle de photo-historien[23]. » Le film ne fut pas un grand succès public, mais il devait marquer de jeunes réalisateurs orientés vers l'ethnographie comme Robert Flaherty (1884–1951), que rendit célèbre son film sur les Inuit *Nanouk l'Esquimau* (1922).

The Morning Bath
Das morgendliche Bad
Le bain du matin
Apache, 1906

state sponsorship, either from the Smithsonian Institution, or from the American Bureau of Ethnology. Established ethnologists and anthropologists regarded Curtis' activities with suspicion. The photographer had no academic training, and yet thanks to his contacts with people in high places and to his skills as a lecturer he was better known than many a professor. The scientists were above all offended by the aesthetic character of his photographs. Curtis wanted to present the fruits of his expeditions in artistic form, and his pictures betrayed an idealized view of reality. The photographer "staged-managed" his models in their surroundings, and was not content with the simple, matter-of-fact directions that documentary photographers normally give to their models, or even reject altogether as a source of distortion.

Ethnologists and anthropologists at American universities wanted to see a strict division between art and science, as a result of which Curtis' texts were rarely reviewed, all the more so because they did not appear in the specialist journals reporting on the latest developments in science. The scientists punished the beautiful but extremely pricey limited edition of *The North American Indian*, as well as the popular magazines that printed Curtis' photos, by ignoring them. In all fairness, however, it should be added that Curtis for his part paid scant attention to other people's researches in this field, which rightly met with consternation.

In the person of Frederick Hodge, however, who was one of the few renowned scientists to support the photographer, Curtis had a seasoned specialist from the American Bureau of Ethnology on his side, albeit in a more private than official function. Hodge became active as Curtis' editor, exerting a positive influence on his project in both word and deed.

Seine Bilder zeugen von einem idealistischen Blick auf die Wirklichkeit. Der Photograph setzte seine Modelle in ihrer Umgebung in Szene und beschränkte sich nicht auf die einfachen, sachlichen Regieanweisungen, die Dokumentarphotographen ihren Modellen üblicherweise geben, wenn sie nicht sogar solche sparsamen Anweisungen als verfälschende Arrangements ablehnen. Die ethnologischen und anthropologischen Wissenschaftler an den amerikanischen Universitäten wollten Kunst und Wissenschaft streng getrennt sehen. Die Folge war, daß auch Curtis' Texte kaum rezipiert wurden, zumal sie nicht in den Fachperiodika erschienen, die über den aktuellen Stand der Wissenschaft berichteten. Die Forscher straften die wunderschöne, jedoch extrem teure limitierte Auflage von *The North American Indian* sowie die populären Magazine, in denen Curtis' Photos erschienen, mit Nichtachtung. Allerdings interessierte sich Curtis auch kaum für die Forschungen anderer, was zu Recht auf Befremden stieß.

Mit Frederick Hodge, einem der wenigen bekannten Wissenschaftler, die Curtis unterstützten, stand dem Photographen jedoch ein erfahrener Spezialist vom American Bureau of Ethnology zur Seite, wenn auch eher in privater als in offizieller Funktion. Hodge wurde als Curtis' Herausgeber tätig und übte mit Rat und Tat positiven Einfluß auf das Projekt aus.

Die Dokumentation der Geschichte aller eingeborenen amerikanischen Populationen, die sich Curtis zum Ziel gesetzt hatte, war ein derart umfangreiches Projekt, daß es selbst bei übermenschlicher Anstrengung zwangsläufig bruchstückhaft und damit angreifbar bleiben mußte. Weil Curtis sich zudem mit einer Vielzahl von Sachgebieten befaßte und sich nicht auf ein einziges konzentrierte, wurde er von weniger universal orientierten Wissenschaftlern kritisiert.

Oft wurde der Photograph als Einzelgänger dargestellt, der die Arbeit einer ganzen Institution zu leisten versuchte. Dieses Bild mag seinen Ursprung

Ce n'est qu'à une date récente qu'on commença à découvrir l'importance de Curtis en tant qu'auteur et historien ayant étudié les différentes tribus indiennes. Mais déjà à son époque, le projet de Curtis rencontra des réactions diverses. Malgré le soutien politique de Roosevelt, celui de la Smithsonian Institution tout comme celui de l'American Bureau of Ethnology lui furent refusés. L'activité de Curtis était suspecte aux ethnologues et anthropologues établis. Le photographe en effet ne pouvait justifier d'aucune formation universitaire mais grâce à ses contacts avec des personnalités haut placées et ses talents de conférencier, il était plus connu que bien des professeurs. Les scientifiques prirent essentiellement ombrage du caractère artistique de ses photographies. Curtis voulait que les résultats de ses expéditions soient présentés sous une forme artistique, et la réalité qu'il montre dans ses images est une réalité idéalisée. Le photographe, qui mettait en scène ses modèles dans leur environnement, ne se limitait pas dans ses directives à de simples et sobres indications, comme il est d'usage en photographie documentaire, encore que la notion même de «directives» soit très controversée, voire synonyme de falsification. Les ethnologues et anthropologues des universités américaines voulaient voir une franche séparation entre l'art et la science. A la suite de quoi les textes de Curtis ne trouvèrent, eux non plus, presque aucun accueil, d'autant qu'ils n'avaient pas paru dans les périodiques spécialisés qui faisaient le point sur l'état actuel de la science. Les scientifiques sanctionnèrent de leur indifférence l'édition, superbe mais extrêmement coûteuse du fait de son tirage limité, des *North American Indian*, ainsi que les magazines populaires dans lesquels paraissaient les photos de Curtis. Il faut toutefois reconnaître qu'en contrepartie, Curtis s'intéressait à peine aux recherches des autres, ce qui à raison provoqua des manifestations d'inimitié. Avec Frederick Hodge, l'un des rares scientifiques connus à avoir soutenu Curtis, le photographe avait toutefois à ses côtés un spécialiste expérimenté

The aim that Curtis set himself, to document the history of all the indigenous American peoples, was such an extensive project that even with superhuman efforts it would necessarily have remained fragmentary and open to criticism. Moreover, since Curtis addressed a number of different subjects rather than concentrating on one alone, he was criticized by scientists with a less universalist orientation.

The photographer was often depicted as a lone wolf trying to accomplish the work of an entire institution. This image may well have had its origins in the way Curtis presented himself in public. Yet he by no means conducted his researches on his own, but rather apportioned the core areas of the work among a team of up to 17 collaborators. Curtis organized and coordinated each phase of the project, wrote and edited part of the texts, and took all the photographs. His staff not only worked with him in the field during the travelling season, but also collaborated with him in various cities scattered throughout the USA: in the photographic studio in Seattle, selling books in New York, and at the publisher's in Washington.

William E. Myers, an expert stenographer and a gifted phonetician, acted as Curtis' right-hand man in the field. Whenever Curtis conducted interviews, Myers and an interpreter sat at his side. Myers would write down the most important information in shorthand, and immediately draw Curtis' attention to anything he forgot. The efficiency of this system, together with an average of sixteen hours of work a day, enabled the comprehensive corpus of material to be gathered. As soon as enough information had been collected on a tribe, Myers and Curtis would withdraw to a mountain cabin and in long cloistered sessions work out the final version of the text. William Myers wrote large sections of the first eighteen volumes of *The North American Indian* by himself, and as

darin haben, wie Curtis sich in der Öffentlichkeit präsentierte. Er führte seine Forschungen jedoch keinesfalls allein durch, sondern teilte die Arbeitsschwerpunkte innerhalb eines Teams von bis zu 17 Mitarbeitern auf. Curtis organisierte und koordinierte sämtliche Projektphasen, er schrieb und edierte einen Teil der Texte und nahm alle Photographien auf. Seine Mitarbeiter arbeiteten nicht nur während der Reisesaison im Feld, sondern wirkten verstreut über die USA an verschiedenen Orten an dem Projekt mit: im Photoatelier in Seattle, als Buchverkäufer in New York und als Herausgeber in Washington.

William E. Myers, ein Meister der Stenographie und zugleich in der phonetischen Umschrift talentiert, war Curtis' Assistent während der Feldforschungen. Wenn Curtis Interviews führte, saßen Myers und ein Dolmetscher stets an seiner Seite. Myers stenographierte die wichtigsten Informationen mit, und wenn Curtis etwas vergaß, machte er ihn direkt darauf aufmerksam. Diese effektive Arbeitsweise und eine durchschnittliche Arbeitszeit von 16 Stunden täglich ermöglichten es, das umfangreiche Material für das ehrgeizige Projekt zusammenzutragen. Sobald genügend Informationen über einen Stamm gesammelt waren, zogen sich Myers und Curtis in die Abgeschiedenheit einer Berghütte zurück und einigten sich in langen Klausuren auf die Endfassung der Manuskripte. William Myers schrieb große Teile der ersten 18 Bände von *The North American Indian* selbständig und hatte als Wissenschaftler großen Anteil am Zustandekommen des Projekts. Dennoch blieb er in der Enzyklopädie – abgesehen von einer kurzen dankenden Erwähnung im Vorwort der Bände – als Autor unerwähnt.

Das Photoatelier in Seattle wurde von dem talentierten Photographen Adolph F. Muhr geleitet. Er bearbeitete auch Curtis' Indianernegative und konnte sich daher dem Studio nur begrenzt widmen, weshalb die Einnahmen, von denen eigentlich Curtis' Familie leben sollte, sanken.

de l'American Bureau of Ethnology, ne fût-ce que dans une fonction davantage privée qu'officielle. Hodge travailla comme éditeur de Curtis et eut, en actes comme en paroles, une influence positive sur le projet.

L'objectif que s'était fixé Curtis de documenter l'histoire de toutes les populations indigènes des Etats-Unis était un projet tellement vaste que même avec des efforts surhumains, il était condamné à rester à l'état de fragments et par là, prêtait le flanc à la critique. Comme, d'autre part, Curtis s'intéressait à une multiplicité de domaines sans en privilégier aucun en particulier, il était très contesté par des scientifiques peu enclins à l'universalité.

On a souvent représenté le photographe comme un individu qui essayait de faire le travail de toute une institution. Cette image trouve peut-être son origine dans la façon qu'avait Curtis de paraître en public. Il n'effectuait pas pour autant ses recherches tout seul, mais répartissait les principales tâches au sein d'une petite équipe de 17 collaborateurs. Curtis organisait et coordonnait l'ensemble des phases du projet, il écrivait et publiait une partie des textes et faisait toutes les photographies. Ses collaborateurs ne travaillaient pas seulement pendant la période passée sur le terrain, mais leur participation au projet se poursuivait de façon dispersée dans plusieurs endroits des Etats-Unis : au studio photo de Seattle, à New York où ils vendaient les ouvrages et à Washington où ils les éditaient.

William E. Myers, excellent sténographe en même temps que phonéticien doué pour les langues, assistait Curtis dans ses recherches sur le terrain. Chaque fois que celui-ci interviewait des gens, Myers et un interprète étaient assis à sa droite. Myers sténographiait les informations les plus importantes et si Curtis oubliait quelque chose, il le lui faisait ouvertement remarquer. Cette façon efficace de travailler ainsi qu'une durée moyenne de 16 heures de travail par jour permirent de rassembler l'impressionnante quantité de matériaux nécessaires à la réalisation de cet ambitieux projet. Dès qu'ils

a scientist played a large part in the realization of the project. And yet he was never named as an author in the encyclopaedia, his only mention being restricted to a brief word of thanks in the foreword to each volume.

The studio in Seattle was managed by the talented photographer Adolph F. Muhr. He also dealt with Curtis' Indian negatives, and thus could only dedicate a limited amount of his time to the studio. As a result, the income from which Curtis' family were supposed to live diminished.

After the first injection of funds from Morgan, Curtis had initially thought that his financial problems were over. Yet his assistants alone cost him up to 4,500 dollars a month in wages, and the field work dragged on for much longer than expected. From the outset, the costs for staff, travelling, production and printing overstepped his budget, despite the revenue he received from picture sales, subscriptions and lectures. All in all the project swallowed roughly one and a half million dollars. [24] In 1909 Morgan helped out with a further 60,000 dollars, but not a year passed in which Curtis could dedicate himself to his project without being plagued by financial worries. This constant shortage of money, along with the photographer's almost permanent absence, led to rows between Curtis and his wife. In 1916 Clara Curtis filed a divorce, and since Edward Curtis neglected to appear before the judge in Seattle until 1918, he was also charged with contempt of court.

Between 1916 and 1922, no further volumes of *The North American Indian* appeared, partly because the paper for printing could not be imported from Europe during the First World War, and partly because the separation from his wife and subsequent drain on his finances, as well as the death of Adolph F. Muhr in 1915, left Curtis physically and financially incapable of continuing his life work.

Nach dem ersten Geldsegen von Morgan hatte Curtis zunächst geglaubt, daß seine finanziellen Probleme gelöst seien, doch allein die Mitarbeiter kosteten bis zu 4500 Dollar pro Monat, und die Feldarbeit zog sich viel länger hin als erwartet. Von Anfang an überstiegen die Kosten für Reisen, Mitarbeiter, Produktion und Druck trotz Bildverkäufen, Subskriptionen und Vorträgen das Budget. Insgesamt verschlang das Projekt rund eineinhalb Millionen Dollar. [24] 1909 half Morgan noch einmal mit 60 000 Dollar aus, und doch verging kein Jahr, in dem Curtis sich ohne finanzielle Sorgen seiner Aufgabe widmen konnte. Die ständige Geldnot sowie die fast permanente Abwesenheit von Edward Curtis führten zum Zerwürfnis zwischen dem Photographen und seiner Frau. 1916 reichte Clara Curtis die Scheidung ein, und weil Edward Curtis bis 1918 nicht vor den Richtern in Seattle erschien, wurde er schließlich sogar wegen Mißachtung des Gerichts angeklagt. Zwischen 1916 und 1922 erschien kein Band von *The North American Indian*, teils weil das Papier für den Druck während des Ersten Weltkriegs nicht aus Europa importiert werden konnten, teils weil Curtis nach seiner Trennung und dem damit verbundenen finanziellen Aderlaß sowie nach Adolph F. Muhrs Tod 1915 weder physisch noch finanziell in der Lage war, sein Lebenswerk fortzusetzen.

1919 zog Curtis nach Los Angeles und nahm in Hollywoods Filmstudios Auftragsarbeiten an. Er arbeitete als Kameramann, und wir wissen, daß er außerdem Standbilder für Cecil B. De Milles (1881–1959) Stummfilm-Epos *Die Zehn Gebote* (1923) aufnahm. Insgesamt ist diese Schaffenszeit in Curtis' Werk jedoch noch nicht detailliert erforscht. Die finanzielle Situation erlaubte es dem Photographen 1922, sein Lebenswerk mit dem zwölften Band von *The North American Indian* fortzusetzen. Auch von der Familie Morgan wurde der Photograph jetzt wieder unterstützt. Pierpont Morgan war bereits 1913 gestorben, doch da die Subskribenten nicht nur bei Curtis, sondern auch

avaient réuni suffisamment d'informations sur une tribu, Myers et Curtis se retiraient et allaient s'isoler dans une cabane de montagne pour convenir, au terme de longs huis clos, de la forme définitive à donner aux manuscrits. William Myers écrivit de grands pans des 18 premiers volumes des *North American Indian* de manière autonome et si le projet put se faire, c'est en grande partie grâce à lui et à sa qualité de scientifique. Et pourtant, à l'exception d'une brève mention de remerciement dans la préface des volumes, il ne figurait pas dans l'encyclopédie en tant qu'auteur.

Le studio photo de Seattle fut confié au photographe talentueux Adolph F. Muhr. Comme celui-ci s'occupait également des négatifs de Curtis, il ne pouvait se consacrer à l'atelier que de façon limitée, ce qui provoqua une chute des revenus devant faire vivre la famille Curtis.

Après cette première manne que représentait l'apport financier de Morgan, Curtis avait d'abord cru qu'il en avait fini avec les problèmes d'argent. Les collaborateurs à eux seuls coûtaient cependant jusqu'à 4500 dollars, et le travail sur le terrain se poursuivit beaucoup plus longtemps que prévu. Dès le début, les frais engendrés par les voyages, les collaborateurs, la production et l'impression dépassèrent les prévisions budgétaires malgré les ventes de photos, les souscriptions et les conférences. Le projet engloutit au total près d'un million et demi de dollars [24]. En 1919, Morgan dut apporter à Curtis une nouvelle aide de 60 000 dollars, mais il ne se passa pas une année sans que celui-ci pût se consacrer à sa tâche à l'abri des problèmes financiers.

Le perpétuel manque d'argent et l'absence quasi permanente de Curtis entraînèrent la séparation du photographe et de son épouse. En 1916, Clara Curtis demanda le divorce et comme Edward Curtis négligea jusqu'en 1918 de comparaître devant le juge de Seattle, il finit même par être accusé de non-respect du tribunal. Entre 1916 et 1922, aucun volume des *North American Indian* ne parut, en partie du fait que, pendant la Première Guerre mondiale,

In 1919 Curtis moved to Los Angeles, where he took on commissions from the Hollywood film studios. He worked as a cameraman, and it is known that he took the stills for Cecil B. De Mille's (1881–1959) silent epic *The Ten Commandments* (1923), but this phase of Curtis' work has yet to be researched in greater detail. The subsequent improvement in his financial circumstances allowed Curtis to continue his life work with the twelfth volume of *The North American Indian*. Renewed support for the photographer also came once again from the Morgan family. Pierpont Morgan had died in 1913, but since the subscribers to the encyclopaedia demanded the missing volumes not only from Curtis, but also from the Morgan family, Pierpont's son John resolved in 1922 once more to cover the printing costs and enable completion of the project.

At this point, however, there was virtually no public or scientific interest in the continuation of Curtis' work. Finishing the project exerted such financial and mental pressure on Curtis that he was completely drained, both physically and emotionally. The Boston bookseller Charles Lauriat took over the none too successful distribution of the remaining volumes and gravures. When the project had finally been concluded, Curtis worked for a number of years on the manuscript of a book with the working title *The Lure of Gold*, which was never published. The photographer died in 1952 at Whittier, California, at the age of 84.

It is hard to do justice to such an extensive and qualitatively heterogeneous body of work as that left by Curtis. Are his Indian photographs documents? Are his pictures with their magical quality truly an echo of an age in which people still lived in harmony with nature?

Curtis attempted with passionate enthusiasm to record a culture threatened by extinction in words and

bei der Familie Morgan die fehlenden Bände einforderten, entschloß sich Pierponts Sohn John 1922, die Druckkosten wieder zu übernehmen und den Abschluß des Projektes zu ermöglichen.

Zu diesem Zeitpunkt war ein öffentliches oder wissenschaftliches Interesse am Fortgang von Curtis' Werk allerdings kaum noch vorhanden. Für den Photographen war mit dem Abschluß des Projekts ein derartig starker finanzieller und psychischer Druck verbunden, daß er sich physisch und emotional völlig erschöpfte. Der Bostoner Buchhändler Charles Lauriat übernahm den nicht sehr erfolgreichen Vertrieb der verbleibenden Bände und Gravüren. Curtis arbeitete nach Abschluß des Projekts über mehrere Jahre am Manuskript eines nie veröffentlichten Buches mit dem Arbeitstitel *Der Lockruf des Goldes*. 1952 starb der Photograph 84jährig in Whittier, Kalifornien.

Es ist schwer, einem so umfangreichen und qualitativ heterogenen Werk wie dem von Curtis Gerechtigkeit widerfahren zu lassen. Sind seine Indianerphotographien Dokumente? Sind seine Bilder mit ihrer magischen Qualität wirklich das Echo einer Zeit, in der Mensch und Natur noch miteinander in Einklang lebten?

Mit Leidenschaft versuchte Curtis in Bild und Wort Zeugnisse einer Kultur festzuhalten, die vom Untergang bedroht war. Zu Beginn des Jahrhunderts betrug die gesamte indianische Population Nordamerikas gerade noch 250 000 Menschen, und erst heute umfaßt sie wieder um die zwei Millionen. Curtis sympathisierte mit den Werten der indianischen Kultur und zeigte eine Welt, die auf den ersten Blick unberührt von der weißen Zivilisation erscheint. Ein zweiter, intensiverer Blick auf Curtis' Bilder offenbart jedoch, daß das Idealbild einer Gesellschaft im friedlichen Urzustand zum Zeitpunkt ihrer Entstehung nicht mehr – oder vielleicht auch nie – der Realität entsprach. Obwohl Curtis sich bemühte, alle Zeugnisse der modernen Gesellschaft von seinen Bildern fernzuhalten, schlichen sich Artefakte in sie ein. Ein

on ne pouvait plus importer de papiers d'imprimerie d'Europe, mais aussi parce qu'à la suite de son divorce, de la saignée financière qu'il occasionna et de la mort d'Adolph F. Muhr, survenue en 1915, Curtis n'était plus en mesure physiquement ni financièrement de poursuivre l'œuvre de sa vie.

Il partit en 1919 pour Los Angeles, où il accepta des commandes des studios cinématographiques d'Hollywood. Il travailla comme cameraman, et nous savons qu'il fut photographe de plateau pour l'épopée muette de Cecil B. De Mille (1881–1959) *Les Dix Commandements* (1923). Mais dans l'ensemble, cette période de l'œuvre de Curtis n'a pas encore été étudiée dans le détail. Sa situation financière autorisait à présent le photographe, qui reçut en effet un nouveau soutien de la famille Morgan, à poursuivre l'œuvre de sa vie avec le volume XII des *North American Indian*. Après la mort de Morgan, survenue dès 1913, les souscripteurs exigèrent non seulement de Curtis, mais également de la famille Morgan les volumes manquants. Aussi son fils John Pierpont se décida-t-il en 1922 à reprendre à sa charge les frais d'impression, ce qui permettait de porter le projet à son terme.

A cette époque, l'intérêt tant public que scientifique pour la poursuite de l'œuvre de Curtis avait toutefois presque disparu. La clôture du projet représentait pour le photographe une telle pression financière et psychique qu'il s'épuisait entièrement. Le libraire Charles Lauriat de Boston prit en charge la commercialisation, qui s'avéra peu couronnée de succès, des volumes et des gravures restants. Le projet terminé, Curtis travailla plusieurs années à un manuscrit provisoirement intitulé *L'appel de l'or*, qui ne fut jamais publié. Le photographe mourut à l'âge de 84 ans à Whittier, en Californie.

Il est très difficile de rendre justice à une œuvre aussi vaste et pourvue de qualités aussi diverses que celle de Curtis. Ses photographies d'Indiens sont-elles des documents ? La magie qui émane de ses images est-elle vraiment l'écho d'une époque où l'homme et la nature vivaient encore en harmonie ?

pictures. At the dawn of the 20th century, the total North American Indian population consisted of no more than 250,000 people, and only now has it once again reached the two million mark. Curtis sympathized with the values of Indian culture and showed a world that at first sight seemed untouched by white civilization. However, a second closer look at his pictures reveals that the idealized image of a society living in a peaceful pristine state no longer corresponded with reality – and perhaps never did. Although Curtis took pains to exclude all evidence of modern society from his images, modern artefacts crept into them. A photograph of two Piegan Indians in the keeping of the Copyright Deposit of the Library of Congress in Washington shows that Curtis would even retouch a photograph in order to be able include it in his encyclopaedia without any evidence of modern civilization. The unretouched picture from the Library of Congress shows that the Indians had placed an alarm clock as a symbol of luxury between themselves, the dial turned towards the camera. On the photogravure included in *The North American Indian*, the alarm clock has been retouched out of the picture (ill. p. 97). Presumably Curtis had not insisted on the object being removed at the time of the exposure out of respect for his hosts, but wished to see it eliminated in his publication. Other cases are known in which Curtis resorted to various means to obtain the results he wanted. Some dances and ceremonies were organized specially for his camera. He even gave one medicine man 500 dollars in order to be able to photograph the ceramic figures of the "Holy Turtle" without the other members of the tribe knowing. He paid the Zuñis a fee of 50 cents per pose, which at that time represented half a day's wages.

The way in which Curtis trod a fine line between manipulation, personal interest and the resistance of the

Photo von zwei Piegan-Indianern aus dem Copyright-Deposit der Library of Congress in Washington beweist, daß Curtis auch die Retusche einsetzte, um ein Bild in seiner Enzyklopädie ohne Hinweis auf die moderne Zivilisation zeigen zu können. Das unretuschierte Bild zeigt, daß die Indianer als Zeichen des Luxus einen Wecker zwischen sich postiert haben, dessen Zifferblatt der Kamera zugewandt ist. Auf der Photogravüre des Negativs, die in *The North American Indian* veröffentlicht wurde, ist der Wecker wegretuschiert (Abb. S. 97). Wahrscheinlich hatte Curtis aus Respekt vor seinen Gastgebern nicht darauf gedrungen, den Gegenstand zu entfernen, wollte ihn in seiner Publikation jedoch eliminiert sehen.

Es ist bekannt, daß Curtis auch in anderen Fällen verschiedene Mittel einsetzte, um bestimmte Ergebnisse zu erzielen. Manche Tänze und Zeremonien wurden eigens für die Kamera arrangiert. Einem Medizinmann zahlte er gar 500 Dollar, um die Keramikfiguren der »heiligen Schildkröten« ohne Wissen der anderen Stammesangehörigen photographieren zu können. Die Zuñi entlohnte er mit 50 Cent pro Pose, was zu jener Zeit etwa einem halben Tageslohn entsprach.

Inwieweit Curtis im Spannungsfeld zwischen indianischem Widerstand, Manipulation und Eigeninteressen mit mehr oder minder pekuniärer Überzeugungskraft agierte, läßt ein Artikel in der *Seattle Sunday Times* von 1904 erahnen.[25] Curtis interessierte sich für den Yabachi-Tanz, einen geheimen Ritus der Navaho, den noch niemand im Bild festgehalten hatte. Durch Vermittlung des Leiters eines Handelspostens in Arizona konnte der Photograph 14 Navaho-Tänzer gewinnen, die sich unter strengster Geheimhaltung mehrere Tage mit ihm zurückzogen und ihm den Tanz vorführten. Die Herstellung der Masken, die normalerweise die neun Tage andauernde Zeremonie einleitete, mußte Curtis übernehmen, denn für die Indianer hätte dies eine Sünde bedeutet. Curtis' Aufnahmen des Ritus und die Porträts der Masken-

Curtis a tenté avec passion de fixer par l'image et le texte les témoignages d'une culture menacée de disparition. Au début du siècle, la population indienne totale était encore tout juste de 250 000 personnes, et ce n'est qu'aujourd'hui qu'elle en compte à nouveau dans les deux millions. Curtis, qui sympathisait avec les valeurs de la culture indienne, montrait un monde qui, à première vue, ne semblait pas touché par la civilisation blanche. En y regardant de plus près, on s'aperçoit que cette image idéale d'une société dont le mode de vie pacifique était celui des origines, ne répondait déjà plus – l'avait-elle jamais fait ? – à la réalité. Bien que Curtis se soit efforcé d'écarter de ses images tout ce qui pouvait témoigner de la société moderne, certains de ses artefacts s'y sont tout de même glissés. Comme l'atteste une photo de deux Indiens Pigean provenant du dépôt du copyright de la Library of Congress de Washington, Curtis avait recours à la retouche pour pouvoir montrer dans son encyclopédie une photo d'où soit absente toute allusion à la civilisation moderne. L'image non retouchée de la Library of Congress montre que les Indiens avaient posé entre eux un réveil, censé être un produit de luxe, dont le cadran était tourné vers l'appareil. Sur la photogravure tirée du négatif et publiée dans les *North American Indian* une retouche a fait disparaître le réveil (ill. p. 97). Curtis qui, certainement par respect pour ses hôtes, n'avait pas demandé qu'on enlève cet indice de la civilisation à la prise de vue, voulait cependant le voir effacé dans sa publication.

On sait également par d'autres exemples que Curtis était prêt à mettre en œuvre les moyens les plus divers pour obtenir certains résultats. Certaines danses et cérémonies furent arrangées spécialement pour l'appareil photo. Il alla même jusqu'à donner 500 dollars à un sorcier pour pouvoir photographier les figures de céramique des «tortues sacrées» à l'insu des autres membres de la tribu. Il payait les Zunis 50 cents la pose, ce qui à cette époque correspondait environ à une demi-journée de salaire.

Indians by means of more or less pecuniary persuasion can be guessed at from an article in the *Seattle Sunday Times* from 1904.[25] Curtis was interested in the Yebichai Dance, a secret ritual performed by the Navajo which no one had previously managed to photograph. With the assistance of the manager of a trading post in Arizona, the photographer was able to find fourteen Navajo dancers who, under a cloak of great secrecy, allowed themselves to be shut away with him for several days, where they performed the dance. Curtis had to attend to the process of making the masks, which normally introduced the nine-day ceremony, for otherwise the Indians would have committed a sin. Curtis' pictures of the rite and his portraits of the masked participants are among his most fascinating images, even if this story divests them of some of their authenticity.

This example should not, however, allow one to draw conclusions about the origins of his work as a whole. The majority of Curtis' photographs were taken on location during his expeditions. Over the years, Curtis had developed a exceptional capacity for understanding. "Curtis went to the Indians as man to brother – man for the sake of all men. He went warmly and kindly, with straight looks and honest purpose, without guile. He never accepted the Indians as alien. He sat in their tipis and beside their fires as a humble equal. He made no secret of his inquisitive purpose, but he was willing to control his research until the right time came along."[26] He must also have had the spiritual capacity to tune into the Indians' myths and rites, for the Indians allowed him to participate in many of their ceremonies and to take numerous impressive photographs. With time, the Indian tribes became convinced that Curtis was one of the very few whites to share with them the knowledge of Manitou, the "Great Mystery."

träger gehören zu seinen faszinierendsten Bildern, auch wenn sie angesichts dieser Vorgeschichte an Authentizität verlieren.

Allerdings darf man anhand dieses Beispiels keine Rückschlüsse auf die Entstehung des Gesamtwerkes ziehen. Der Großteil der Aufnahmen entstand auf Curtis' Expeditionen vor Ort. Der Photograph hatte im Laufe der Jahre ein außergewöhnliches Einfühlungsvermögen entwickelt. »Curtis wandte sich an die Indianer wie ein Mann an seinen Bruder [...]. Er war warm und herzlich, geraden Blickes, ehrlichen Herzens und ohne Verstellung. Er betrachtete die Indianer nie als Fremde. Er verstand sich als einer der ihren und saß bescheiden mit ihnen in den Tipis und am Feuer. Aus seiner Neugier machte er kein Geheimnis, aber er war willens, auf den richtigen Zeitpunkt für seine Fragen zu warten.«[26] Er muß auch geistig in der Lage gewesen sein, sich auf die Riten und Mythen der Indianer einzustellen, denn sie ließen ihn an vielen ihrer Zeremonien teilhaben, und so gelangen ihm zahlreiche eindrucksvolle Aufnahmen. Unter den Indianerstämmen verbreitete sich über die Jahre allmählich die Überzeugung, Curtis teile als einer der ganz wenigen Weißen mit ihnen Manitou, das »Große Mysterium«.

Matilda Cox Stevenson, die für das Bureau of American Ethnology arbeitete, lobt in einem Brief an den Photographen sein besonderes Einfühlungsvermögen: »Es ist ein beständiges Wunder für mich, daß Sie in so wenigen Jahren die inneren Türen so vieler Stämme durchschritten haben. Aus meiner eigenen langjährigen Erfahrung mit eingeborenen Völkern lese ich Seiten in Ihrem Werk, die so noch nicht aufgeschlagen worden sind: eine Einsicht in Charakter und Lebensumstände der Indianer; große Nachdrücklichkeit, Mut, Durchhaltevermögen und die große Liebe zur Wahrheit, ohne die wir keine solche Aufzeichnungen wie die Ihren hätten.«[27]

»Als Außenstehende sollten wir uns davor hüten, die Indianer allein nach unseren Normen zu beurteilen, statt ihre eigenen Sitten und Gebräuche zu

Quant à savoir quelle était la marge de manœuvre de Curtis entre la résistance des Indiens, la manipulation et des intérêts personnels servis par une force de persuasion plus ou moins étayée de promesses lucratives, un article du *Seattle Sunday Times* de 1904[25] le laisse entrevoir. Curtis s'intéressait à la danse Yabachi, un rite secret des Navaho que personne n'avait encore photographié. Par l'entremise du chef d'un poste de commerce d'Arizona, le photographe réussit à gagner 14 danseurs navaho qui, dans le plus grand secret, se retirèrent plusieurs jours avec lui et lui présentèrent cette danse. Curtis dut prendre en charge la réalisation des masques, qui normalement inaugurait les 9 jours que durait la cérémonie, car pour les Indiens cela aurait constitué une faute. Les photos qu'il a prises de ce rite ainsi que ses portraits des porteurs de masques comptent parmi les images les plus fascinantes de l'œuvre de Curtis, même si, à partir du moment où l'on connaît ces préliminaires, elles perdent en authenticité.

Il ne faudrait pas pour autant prendre prétexte de cet exemple pour en tirer des conclusions générales sur la genèse de l'œuvre. La majeure partie des photos a été réalisée sur place pendant les expéditions de Curtis. Le photographe avait développé au fil des ans d'extraordinaires capacités intuitives. «Curtis s'adressait aux Indiens comme un homme à son frère [...]. Il était chaleureux et sympathique, avait le regard droit et le cœur franc, sans dissimulation. Il n'a jamais considéré les Indiens comme des étrangers. Il s'asseyait dans leurs tipis et près de leurs feux comme un égal, en toute simplicité. Il ne faisait aucun mystère de sa curiosité, mais il était fermement décidé à attendre le bon moment pour poser ses questions[26].» Sans doute a-t-il également été en mesure de s'adapter aux rites et aux mythes des Indiens, car ceux-ci l'ont fait participer à un grand nombre de leurs cérémonies, ce qui lui a permis de faire une multiplicité de photos impressionnantes. Avec les années, la conviction se répandit peu à peu parmi les tribus indiennes que

Matilda Cox Stevenson, who worked for the Bureau of American Ethnology, praised his powers of empathy in a letter addressed to the photographer: "It is a continual wonder to me that you have in so few years passed within the doors of the inner life of so many tribes. I, from my long experience with native peoples, read pages in your work which are not open at all: a ready insight into the character and conditions of the Indian; great persistency, courage, powers of endurance, and that great love of truth without which we would not today have such records as you have given us."[27]

In *The North American Indian* Curtis writes: "As an alien race, we should hardly presume to judge them wholly by our standards and not give them credit for their own customs and codes. They on their part consider some of our customs highly objectionable and immoral."[28] The quote shows that it would be to misjudge the photographer's work if one were to assess it solely in terms of Curtis' carefully arranged pictures, which have long since become icons, now commanding high prices. The horsemen with their feather headdresses, the women peacefully carrying their pitchers, the close-ups of expressive, often craggy faces – these images are indeed more reminiscent of 19th-century romanticism than of Curtis' own era, in which the first cars were already rolling off the assembly lines.

Through his depiction of the Indians as valiant yet peace-loving peoples who lived in harmony with their families, their tribes, and nature, Curtis might have wanted to make up for the injustices that members of his own race had inflicted on the Indians. He refused to underpin photographically the public view that the poverty-stricken Indians were vegetating as a result of their own weakness, and were antisocial vagabonds.

akzeptieren. Sie betrachten einige unserer Gebräuche ebenfalls als im höchsten Maße befremdlich und unmoralisch."[28] Dieses Zitat von Curtis zeigt, daß man sein Werk falsch einschätzt, wenn man es allein nach seinen sorgfältig arrangierten, inzwischen teuer gehandelten und längst zu Ikonen gewordenen Lichtbildern beurteilt. Die federgeschmückten Reiter, die friedlichen Wasserträgerinnen, die bildfüllenden, ausdrucksstarken, oft faltigen Gesichter erinnern tatsächlich mehr an die Romantik des 19. Jahrhunderts als an Curtis' eigene Zeit, in der ja bereits die ersten Autos vom Fließband liefen.

Vielleicht wollte Curtis durch seine Darstellung der Indianer als streitbare und zugleich friedliebende Menschen, die in Einklang mit Familie, Stamm und Natur lebten, das Unrecht wiedergutmachen, das Angehörige seiner eigenen Rasse an ihnen verübt hatten. Jedenfalls weigerte er sich, die öffentliche Meinung photographisch zu untermauern, die in schrecklicher Armut lebenden Indianer vegetierten aufgrund eigener Schwäche vor sich hin und seien asoziale Vagabunden.

Aufgrund ihrer außerordentlichen Qualität erwecken Curtis' großformatige, ausdrucksstarke Porträtphotos den Eindruck, man könne aus den Bildern Rückschlüsse auf den Charakter der Abgebildeten ziehen – und genau dies scheint Curtis' Intention gewesen zu sein. Hat man nicht den Eindruck, die Indianer würden gleich mit der Erzählung ihrer Lebensgeschichte beginnen? Möchten wir den Menschen mit den wettergegerbten Gesichtern nicht bestimmte Erfahrungen und Eigenschaften zuschreiben? Der Faszination eines guten Photos waren Kritiker zu allen Zeiten erlegen. Sie versuchten, die Gesichter zum Sprechen zu bringen und beschrieben sie doch nur vor dem Hintergrund ihrer persönlichen Überzeugungen und Einschätzungen.

Curtis folgte einem humanistisch-sozialen Denkansatz. Seine Porträts haben den Ureinwohnern des amerikanischen Kontinents, die vom Aussterben bedroht waren, ein Gesicht gegeben. Das Vermächtnis des Photographen

Curtis était un des rares Blancs à partager avec eux le Manitou, le «Grand Mystère».

Dans une lettre qu'elle adresse au photographe, Matilda Cox Stevenson, qui travaillait pour le Bureau of American Ethnology, lui fait compliment de ses facultés d'intuition particulières : «C'est pour moi un prodige permanent de voir que vous avez su, en si peu d'années, franchir les portes intérieures de tant de tribus. Ayant moi-même de longues années d'expérience des peuples indigènes, je lis dans votre œuvre des pages telles qu'on n'en a encore jamais écrites : pénétration du caractère et des conditions de vie des Indiens, énergie, courage, endurance et un grand amour de la vérité, sans lequel nous n'aurions jamais de témoignages de la qualité des vôtres[27].»

«En tant que profanes, nous devrions nous garder de juger les Indiens uniquement d'après nos normes, sans accepter leurs propres usages et coutumes. Ils considèrent de la même façon certaines de nos coutumes comme extrêmement étranges et immorales[28].» Cette citation de Curtis montre qu'on porterait un jugement erroné sur son œuvre si on la mesurait uniquement à ses diapositives soigneusement arrangées, commercialisées entretemps à des prix très élevés et promues depuis longtemps au rang d'icônes. Les cavaliers décorés de plumes, les paisibles porteuses d'eau, les visages, très expressifs et souvent ridés, qui occupent toute la superficie de la photographie rappellent en réalité davantage le romantisme du XIXᵉ siècle que la propre époque de Curtis, époque à laquelle les premières autos sortaient déjà des chaînes de production.

Peut-être Curtis voulait-il, en représentant les Indiens comme des gens à la fois belliqueux et pacifiques vivant en harmonie avec la famille, la tribu et la nature, réparer le tort que leur avaient causé des membres de sa propre race. Quoi qu'il en soit, il refusait de cautionner par ses photographies l'opinion publique selon laquelle les Indiens ne devaient qu'à leur propre faiblesse de

Thanks to their exceptional quality, Curtis' highly expressive large-format portraits give the feeling that one can deduce the subject's character from them – and precisely this seems to have been Curtis' intention. For do they not create the impression that at any moment the Indians will begin to tell the story of their lives? And do we not want to attribute certain experiences and qualities to these people with their weather-beaten faces? Critics from all periods have succumbed to the fascination of a good photograph. Although they attempted to bring the faces to word, ultimately they only ever described them in terms of their own personal convictions and evaluations.

Curtis subscribed to a humanistic, social standpoint. His portraits have given a face to the indigenous peoples of the American continent, who were threatened by extinction. The photographer and researcher's legacy is now carefully preserved in manuscript departments, museums and library stockrooms. At the time it never reached the wide audience that Curtis had hoped for, disappearing for years on end into the bookcases of a small group of bibliophiles. But today his works have imprinted themselves on our minds: pictures of Indians who radiate strength and dignity, pictures that document a great cultural diversity, and pictures that express the universal values of the family, the tribe and the nation. In Curtis' encyclopaedia, the Indian tribes are at last united in peace and brotherhood. His photographs show the Indian heritage and make it a part of American history. The photographs may be posed, idealistic and romantic, but they do represent an American dream, the call for a better world, a dream of pride and freedom.

und Forschers wird heute in Handschriftenabteilungen, Museen und Magazinen bewahrt. Damals erreichte es nicht das große Publikum, das sich Curtis ersehnt hatte, sondern verschwand auf lange Jahre in den Bücherschränken eines kleinen bibliophilen Kreises. Doch heute haben sich seine Arbeiten in unser Gedächtnis eingeprägt: Bilder von Indianern, die Kraft und Würde ausstrahlen, Bilder, die eine große kulturelle Vielfalt dokumentieren, und Bilder, die die universellen Werte der Familie, des Stammes und der Nation zum Ausdruck bringen. In der Enzyklopädie von Curtis sind die Indianerstämme endlich friedlich und brüderlich vereint. Die Photographien zeigen das Erbe der Indianer und machen sie zu einem Teil der amerikanischen Geschichte. Bei allen Einschränkungen stellen sie doch auch einen amerikanischen Traum dar – den von Stolz und Freiheit.

vivre et de végéter dans cette affreuse misère, et qu'ils n'étaient au fond que des vagabonds et des asociaux.

En raison de leur qualité exceptionnelle, les portraits expressifs et en grand format de Curtis éveillent l'impression qu'on pourrait en tirer des conclusions sur le caractère des personnes représentées – et c'est précisément ce qui semble avoir été son intention. Ne croirait-on pas que les Indiens vont se mettre à raconter leur histoire ? N'avons-nous pas envie d'attribuer certaines expériences et certaines qualités à ces êtres aux visages burinés par les conditions climatiques ? A toutes les époques, même les plus diverses, les critiques ont succombé à la fascination d'une bonne photo. Ils ont essayé de faire parler ces visages et pourtant, ils n'ont fait que les décrire à partir de leurs opinions et convictions personnelles.

Le travail de Curtis avait des prémisses d'ordre social et humaniste. Ses portraits ont donné un visage à ces premiers habitants du continent américain que menaçait la disparition. L'œuvre du photographe et chercheur est aujourd'hui conservée dans les départements des manuscrits de certaines bibliothèques, dans des musées et des magazines. Elle ne touchait pas à l'époque le grand public que Curtis avait ardemment désiré atteindre, et elle disparut pendant de longues années dans les bibliothèques d'un petit cercle de bibliophiles. Mais ses travaux se sont aujourd'hui gravés dans nos mémoires, des images d'Indiens qui dégagent une impression de force et de dignité, des images qui illustrent une grande diversité culturelle, des images enfin qui expriment les valeurs universelles de la famille, de la tribu et de la nation. Dans l'encyclopédie de Curtis, les tribus indiennes sont enfin unies dans la paix et la fraternité. Ces photographies montrent l'héritage des Indiens, dont elles font une partie de l'histoire de l'Amérique. Quelles que soient les réserves qu'on puisse leur opposer, elles représentent, elles aussi, un rêve américain, un rêve de fierté et de liberté.

The Vanishing Race
A Picture by Edward S. Curtis

Into the shadows, whose illumined crest
Speaks of the world behind them where the sun
Still shines for us whose day is not yet done,
Those last dark ones go drifting. East or West,
Or North or South – it matters not; their quest
Is toward the shadows whence it was begun;
Hope in it, Ah, my brothers! there is none;
And yet – they only seek a place to rest.

So mutely, uncomplainingly, they go!
How shall it be with us when they are gone,
When they are but a mem'ry and a name?
May not those mournful eyes to phantoms grow –
When, wronged and lonely, they have drifted on
Into the voiceless shadow whence they came?

Ella Higginson (1860s–1940)

The Vanishing Race
Die aussterbende Rasse
Une race qui s'éteint
Navaho, 1904

Vash Gon
Jicarilla, 1904

A Son of the Desert
Ein Sohn der Wüste
Un fils du désert
Navaho, 1904

Apache Nalin, 1903

Nez Percé Baby, 1900
Säugling bei den Nez Percé
Bébé Nez Percé

Nature's Mirror
Ein natürlicher Spiegel
Le miroir de la nature
Navaho, 1904

The Blanket Weaver
Die Deckenweberin
La tisseuse de couverture
Navaho, 1904

Giving the Medicine
Verabreichung von Medizin
L'administration des remèdes
Navaho, 1905

Yebichai Sweat
Schwitzbad des Yebichai
Bain de sueur du Yébichai
Navaho, 1904

Apache Medicine-Man, 1907
Apache-Medizinmann
Sorcier apache

The Medicine-Man (Slow Bull), 1907
Der Medizinmann (Slow Bull)
Le Sorcier (Slow Bull)

Tobadzischíni
Navaho, 1904

Haschebaád
Navaho, 1904

Haschógan
Navaho, 1904

Haschezhini
Navaho, 1904

Zahadolzhá
Navaho, 1904

Gánaskidi
Navaho, 1904

A Painted Tipi
Bemaltes Tipi
Un tipi peint
Assiniboin, 1926

X2327-07

Qahátika Girl, 1907
Qahátikamädchen
Jeune fille Qahátika

Ben Long Ear, 1905

Hupa Woman, 1923
Hupafrau
Femme Hupa

Wife of Modoc Henry
Modoc Henrys Frau
Femme de Modoc Henry
Klamath, 1923

Mósa
Mohave, 1903

Kiho Carrier
»Kiho«-Korbträgerin
Porteuse de panier « kiho »
Qahátika, 1907

Gathering Hánamh
Kakteenfruchtsammlerin
Cueillette du Hánamh
Papago, 1907

Women at Campfire
Frauen am Lagerfeuer
Femmes autour d'un feu de camp
Apache, 1903

At the Ford
An der Furt
Le gué
Apache, 1903

Jerking Meat
Herstellung von Dörrfleisch
Dépecage de la viande
Flathead, 1910

Drying Meat
Fleisch wird getrocknet
Séchage de la viande
Sioux, 1908

A Winter Day
Ein Wintertag
Journée d'hiver
Apsaroke, 1908

Winter
Winter
Hiver
Apsaroke, 1908

American Horse
Oglala (Teton Sioux), 1908

Brulé Sioux War Party, 1907
Kriegergruppe der Brulé
Bande de guerriers brulés

Ready for the Charge
Bereit zum Angriff
Prêt à charger
Apsaroke, 1908

In the original photo (above), an alarm clock has been placed as a symbol of luxury between Little Plume and his son Yellow Kidney. Wanting to eliminate any trace of modern civilization from "The North American Indian", Curtis carefully retouched the photograph for the encyclopaedia.

Auf dem Originalphoto (oben) ist zwischen Little Plume und seinem Sohn Yellow Kidney als Zeichen des Luxus ein Wecker plaziert. Da Curtis in »The North American Indian« jeglichen Hinweis auf die moderne Zivilisation ausblenden wollte, hat er die Photographie für die Enzyklopädie sorgfältig retuschiert.

Sur la photo originale (en haut), un réveil est placé entre Little Plume et son fils Yellow Kidney pour symboliser le luxe. Mais comme Curtis voulait éviter toute allusion à la civilisation moderne dans « The North American Indian », il a soigneusement retouché cette photo pour l'encyclopédie.

Unretouched photo, Library of Congress
Unretuschiertes Photo
Photo non retouchée

Lodge Interior
Das Innere eines Tipis
L'intérieur d'un tipi
Piegan, 1910

Retouched photo, The North American Indian
Retuschiertes Photo
Photo retouchée

Weasel Tail
Piegan, 1900

Crazy Thunder
Oglala (Teton Sioux), 1907

For Strength and Visions
Um Kraft und Visionen zu erlangen
Pour la force et les visions
Apsaroke, 1908

The Oath
Der Eid
Le serment
Apsaroke, 1908

Crying to the Spirits, 1908
Die Geister werden angerufen
Invocation des esprits

Incense over a Medicine Bundle
Weihrauch über einem Medizinbündel
Encens au-dessus d'une préparation médicinale
Hidatsa, 1908

The Eagle Medicine-Man
Der Adler-Medizinmann
Le Sorcier aigle
Apsaroke, 1908

The Eagle-Catcher, 1908
Der Adlerfänger
Le chasseur d'aigle

An Oasis in the Bad Lands, South Dakota, 1905
Eine Oase in den Badlands, Süddakota
Une oasis dans les Bad Lands, Dakota du Sud

In the Bad Lands, South Dakota, 1904
In den Badlands, Süddakota
Dans les Bad Lands, Dakota du Sud

Bear's Belly
Arikara, 1908

Arikara Medicine Ceremony · The Bears, 1908
Ritual der Bruderschaft der Medizinmänner · Die Bären
Cérémonie de médecine Arikara · Les Ours

Hide Scraping
Eine Tierhaut wird abgeschabt
Echarnage d'une peau d'animal
Apsaroke, 1908

Moss for the Baby-Bags
Torfmoos für die Babytragen
Mousse destinée aux sacs dans lesquels on porte les enfants
Cree, 1926

Woman's Costume and Baby Swing
Eine Frau im traditionellen Gewand und eine Babyschaukel
Costume de femme et balançoire d'enfant
Assiniboin, 1926

Cheyenne Child, 1927
Kind der Cheyenne
Enfant Cheyenne

Wishram Bride, 1910
Braut bei den Wishram
Mariée Wishram

Wishram Child, 1909
Kind der Wishram
Enfant Wishram

Apsaroke Girl, 1905
Apsarokemädchen
Jeune fille Apsaroke

Playmates
Spielgefährten
Camarades de jeu
Apsaroke, 1905

Wolf
Apsaroke, 1908

A Typical Nez Percé, 1910
Ein typischer Vertreter der Nez Percé
Un Nez Percé typique

Woista · Cheyenne Woman, 1927
Cheyennefrau
Femme Cheyenne

Bull Chief
Apsaroke, 1908

A Medicine-Pipe
Eine Medizinpfeife
Une pipe à usage médicinal
Piegan, 1910

Shot in the Hand
Apsaroke, 1908

Hollow Horn Bear
Brulé Sioux, 1907

New Chest
Piegan, 1910

Arikara Medicine Ceremony · Night Men Dancing, 1908
Medizinzeremonie der Arikara · die Bruderschaft der Männer der Nacht beim Tanz
Cérémonie de médecine Arikara · Danse des hommes de la Nuit

Arikara Medicine Ceremony · The Ducks, 1908
Medizinzeremonie der Arikara · Die Enten
Cérémonie de médecine Arikara · Les Canards

The Rush Gatherer
Die Binsensammlerin
La cueilleuse de joncs
Kutenai, 1910

A Flathead Dance, 1910
Ein Tanz der Flathead
Danse Flathead

The Chief
Der Häuptling
Le Chef
Klamath, 1923

Flathead Warrior, 1910
Krieger der Flathead
Guerrier Flathead

Head Carry
Plateau, 1900

Placating the Spirit of a Slain Eagle
Der Geist eines getöteten Adlers wird besänftigt
Apaisement de l'esprit d'un aigle tué
Assiniboin, 1926

Cheyenne Warriors, 1905
Krieger der Cheyenne
Guerriers Cheyennes

On Spokane River, 1910
Am Spokane-Fluß
Sur la rivière Spokane

Chief Joseph
Häuptling Joseph
Le Chef Joseph
Nez Percé, 1903

Chief Joseph
Häuptling Joseph
Le Chef Joseph
Nez Percé, 1903

A Drink
Eine Erfrischung
Rafraîchissement
Flathead, 1910

Flathead Childhood, 1910
Kindheit bei den Flathead
Enfance Flathead

Canoe of Tules
Kanu aus Sumpfbinsen
Canoë de joncs
Pomo, 1924

By the Pool · Tule River Reservation, 1924
Am Teich · Tule-River-Reservat
Près du bassin · Réserve de Tule River

Watching the Dancers (Walpi)
Ein Blick auf die Tänzer (Walpi)
En regardant les danseurs (Walpi)
Hopi, 1906

Chaiwa-Tewa-Profile, 1921
Ein Chaiwa-Tewa-Profil
Profil Chaiwa-Tewa

Chaiwa-Tewa, 1921

Walpi Maidens
Unverheiratete Mädchen aus Walpi
Jeunes filles de Walpi
Hopi, 1906

Counting the Record, Middle Mesa
Zählen der Verluste, Zweite Mesa
L'inventaire des pertes ennemies, Middle Mesa
Hopi, 1921

Piki Bread Maker, 1903
Pikibrot-Bäckerin
Préparation du pain piki

Hopi Melon Eaters, or "The Delights of Childhood", 1900
Melonenesser bei den Hopi oder »Die Freuden der Kindheit«
Mangeurs de melon Hopi ou « Les délices de l'enfance »

Hopi Melon Eaters, or "The Delights of Childhood", 1900
Melonenesser bei den Hopi oder »Die Freuden der Kindheit«
Mangeurs de melon Hopi ou « Les délices de l'enfance »

Singing to the Snakes
Gesang für die Schlangen
Charmeurs de serpents
Shipaulovi, 1906

Snakes and Antelopes at Oraibi, 1921
Antilopen und Schlangen in Oraibi
Antilopes et Serpents à Oraibi

Snake Dancer and "Hugger", 1921
Schlangentänzer und »Hugger«
Danseur de la Danse du Serpent et « Hugger »

A Snake Priest of the Antelope Fraternity
Ein Schlangenpriester der Antilopen-Bruderschaft
Prêtre du Serpent appartenant à la confrérie de l'Antilope
Hopi, 1921

Awaiting the Return of the Snake Racers
Die Rückkehr der Schlangenläufer wird erwartet
En attendant le retour des coureurs de serpents
Hopi, 1921

A Walpi Man
Walpi-Mann
Un homme Walpi
Hopi, 1921

A Load of Fuel
Eine Fuhre Brennmaterial
Chargement de combustible
Zuñi, 1903

Tsi'yoné ("Flying")
Sia, 1925

Taos Water Girls, 1905
Wassermädchen aus Taos
Porteuses d'eau de Taos

At the Old Well of Acoma, 1904
Am alten Brunnen von Acoma
Au vieux puits d'Acoma

Acoma Water Girls, 1904
Wassermädchen von Acoma
Porteuses d'eau d'Acoma

A Paguate Entrance, 1925
Eingang zu einem Paguate
Entrée d'une maison Paguate

Tápâ ("Antelope Water")
Taos, 1905

Taos Children, 1905
Kinder aus Taos
Enfants de Taos

Hopi Children, 1905
Hopikinder
Enfants Hopi

Acoma Belfry, 1904
Glockenstube in Acoma
Clocher d'Acoma

A Feast Day at Acoma, 1904
Ein Feiertag in Acoma
Jour de fête à Acoma

Acoma Roadway, 1904
Straße in Acoma
Route d'Acoma

Old Trail at Acoma, 1904
Alter Pfad in Acoma
Ancienne piste à Acoma

Tablita Woman Dancer
Tablitatänzerin
Danseuse Tablita
San Ildefonso, 1905

Okúwa-tsiré ("Cloud-bird")
San Ildefonso, 1905

Offering to the Sun
Das Sonnenopfer
Offrande au soleil
San Ildefonso, 1925

Eagle Dancer
Adlertänzer
Danseur aigle
San Ildefonso, 1925

The Bowman, 1915
Der Bogenschütze
L'archer

Masked Dancer
Tänzer mit Maske
Danseur masqué
Cowichan, 1912

Hupa Female Shaman, 1923
Schamanin der Hupa
Femme chaman Hupa

Klamath Woman, 1923
Klamathfrau
Femme Klamath

Lélehalt
Quilcene, 1912

Tsátsalatsa
Skokomish, 1912

Tsawatenok Girl, 1914
Tsawatenokmädchen
Jeune fille Tsawatenok

Quilcene Boy, 1912
Quilcenejunge
Jeune garçon Quilcene

Wishram Maid, 1909
Unverheiratete Wishram
Jeune fille Wishram

The Fisherman
Der Fischer
Le pêcheur
Wishram, 1909

Ceremonial Bathing of Female Shaman
Das zeremonielle Bad einer Schamanin
Ablutions rituelles d'une femme chaman
Clayoquot, 1915

Woman Shaman Looking for Clairvoyant Visions
Schamanin in Erwartung einer Vision
Femme chaman attendant des visions
Clayoquot, 1915

Costume of a Woman Shaman
Kleidung einer Schamanin
Costume d'une femme chaman
Clayoquot, 1915

The Whaler, 1915
Der Walfänger
Le baleinier

The Captured Whale
Der gefangene Wal
La baleine capturée
Neah Bay, 1915

Halibut Fishers
Heilbuttfischer
Pêcheurs de flétans
Neah Bay, 1915

The Whaler
Der Walfänger
Le baleinier
Makah, 1915

It was thought that an eclipse of the moon was caused by some celestial creature attempting to swallow the heavenly body. To stop the monster doing so, people danced round a smouldering fire of old clothing and hair, the stench of which would so irritate the monster's nostrils that it would have to sneeze the moon out again.

Man glaubte, eine Mondfinsternis entsteht dadurch, daß ein überirdisches Wesen versucht, den Himmelskörper zu verschlucken. Um das Monster davon abzuhalten, tanzen die Menschen um ein schwelendes Feuer aus alten Kleidungsstücken und Haaren, dessen Gestank die Nüstern des Wesens so reizt, daß es niesen muß und den Mond wieder ausspeit.

L'éclipse de lune est considérée comme la tentative d'un être surnaturel d'avaler le corps céleste. Afin de l'obliger à le recracher, le peuple danse autour d'un feu alimenté de vieux vêtements et de poils et dont on espère que la puanteur, en montant jusqu'à ses narines, fera éternuer le monstre et libérera l'astre emprisonné.

Dancing to Restore an Eclipsed Moon
Tanz zur Wiedererlangung des Mondes nach einer Mondfinsternis
Danse pour ramener une lune éclipsée
Qágyuhl, 1914

Masked Dancers
Maskierte Tänzer
Danseurs masqués
Qágyuhl, 1914

Coming for the Bride
Die Braut wird geholt
En route vers la mariée
Qágyuhl, 1914

Group of Winter Dancers
Eine Gruppe von Wintertänzern
Groupe de danseurs de l'hiver
Qágyuhl, 1914

Kalóqutsuis
Qágyuhl, 1914

Grizzly Bear Dancer
Qágyuhl, 1914

Wáswaslikyi
Qágyuhl, 1914

Tawihyilahl
Qágyuhl, 1914

Hamasilahl
Qágyuhl, 1914

A Nakoaktok Máwihl, 1914
Ein Máwihl der Nakoaktok
Un Máwihl Nakoaktok

Qúnhunahl
Qágyuhl, 1914

A Tlu'wulahu Mask
Eine Tlu'wulahu-Maske
Masque Tlu'wulahu
Tsawatenok, 1914

A Hamatsa Costume
Ein Hamatsa-Kostüm
Costume Hamatsa
Nakoaktok, 1914

The Drying Mummy
Die Mumie
Momie
Qágyuhl, 1914

Kominaka Dancer
Kominakatänzer
Danseur Kominaka
Kwakiutl, 1914

Kwakiutl House Frame, 1914
Balkenwerk eines Kwakiutl-Hauses
Charpente de maison Kwakiutl

A Haida Chief's Tomb at Yan, 1915
Das Grabmal eines Haida-Häuptlings in Yan
Tombe de chef Haida à Yan

A Nootka, 1915

Chief's Daughter
Häuptlingstochter
Fille d'un Chef Skokomish
Skokomish, 1912

Painting a Hat
Das Bemalen eines Huts
Peinture d'un chapeau
Nakoaktok, 1914

A Nakoaktok Chief's Daughter, 1914
Häuptlingstochter der Nakoaktok
Fille d'un Chef Nakoaktok

Woman and Child
Mutter mit Kind
Femme et enfant
Nunivak, 1928

Ceremonial Mask
Zeremonienmaske
Masque de cérémonie
Nunivak, 1928

Ready for the Throw
Zum Wurf bereit
Prêt pour le lancer
Nunivak, 1928

Óla
Noatak, 1928

Noatak Child, 1929
Kind der Noatak
Enfant Noatak

Biography
Biographie
Biographie

1868

Edward Sheriff Curtis is born on 16 February on a farm in Cold Springs, Jefferson County, Wisconsin, as the second of four children of the preacher Johnson Curtis and his wife, Ellen Sheriff Curtis.

ca. 1885

After teaching himself the rudiments of photography, Edward Curtis becomes an apprentice in a photo studio in St. Paul, Minnesota.

1887

Edward moves with his family to Sidney in Washington State, where his ailing father dies the following year.

Edward S. Curtis, 1951
Photographer unknown
Photograph unbekannt
Photographe inconnu

1868

Edward Sheriff Curtis wird am 16. Februar auf einer Farm in Cold Springs, Jefferson County, Wisconsin, als zweites von vier Kindern des Predigers Johnson und seiner Frau Ellen Sheriff Curtis geboren.

ca. 1885

Nachdem Edward Curtis zuvor autodidaktisch erste Erfahrung auf dem Gebiet der Photographie gesammelt hat, wird er Lehrling in einem Photostudio in St. Paul, Minnesota.

1887

Mit seiner Familie zieht Edward nach Sidney im Staate Washington, wo der kranke Vater im Jahr darauf stirbt.

ca. 1892

Edward Curtis wird Partner im Photostudio von Rasmus Rothi in Seattle, Washington.

1892

Der Photograph heiratet Clara Phillips. Verschiedene Mitglieder der Familien Curtis und Phillips arbeiten in den folgenden Jahren in Edwards Photogeschäft mit.

1893

Curtis wird Partner im Atelier von Thomas Guptil.

1895/96

Am Puget Sound und in der nahe Seattle gelegenen Tulahip Reservation nimmt der Photograph erste Indianerporträts auf.

1897

Edward Curtis macht sich selbständig und firmiert unter »Edward S. Curtis, Photographer and Photoengraver«, wobei er das Gravurgeschäft bald wieder aufgibt. Curtis wird zum führenden Gesellschaftsphotographen in Seattle und genießt auch national

Curtis' studio on 4th Avenue and University Street,
Seattle, Washington, ca. 1918
Das Studio von Curtis an der 4. Avenue und University Street in Seattle, Washington
Le Studio Curtis sur la 4ᵉ Avenue et University Street à Seattle

1868

Naissance le 16 février d'Edward Sheriff Curtis dans un ranch de Cold Springs, Jefferson County, Wisconsin. Il est le second des quatre enfants du prédicateur Johnson et de son épouse Ellen Sheriff Curtis.

ca. 1885

Après avoir acquis en autodidacte une première expérience photographique, il apprend les rudiments de la photographie dans un studio de St. Paul, Minnesota.

1887

Edward s'installe avec sa famille à Sidney, dans l'Etat de Washington, où son père malade décède l'année suivante.

ca. 1892

Edward Curtis devient associé du studio photo de Rasmus Rothi à Seattle, Washington.

On Custer's Outlook – Crow
Curtis, 2nd from right, with Crow scouts, 1908
Auf Custers Aussichtspunkt – Crow
Curtis sitzt als Zweiter von rechts zwischen den Crow-Scouts
Point de vue de Custer – Crow
Curtis, 2ᵉ à partir de la droite, avec des éclaireurs Crow

Rabindranath Tagore (1861–1941), 1916
*The Indian poet, philosopher and Nobel Prize
laureate, photographed by the Curtis Studio
in Seattle*
*Der indische Dichter, Philosoph und Nobel-
preisträger wurde im Studio von Curtis in Seattle
porträtiert*
*Le poëte et philosophe indien lauréat du Prix Nobel,
photographié par le Studio Curtis de Seattle*

ca. 1892
Edward Curtis becomes a partner in the photo studio run by Rasmus Rothi in Seattle, Washington.

1892
The photographer marries Clara Phillips. Various members of the Curtis and Phillips families work in Curtis' photographic business over the coming years.

1893
Curtis becomes a partner in Thomas Guptil's studio.

1895/96
Curtis takes his first Indian portrait at Puget Sound and in the Tulahip Reservation near Seattle.

1897
Edward Curtis sets himself up as a self-employed "Photographer and Photoengraver", as he refers to himself, but soon drops the engraving side of his

einen Ruf als anerkannter Porträtist. Darüber hinaus widmet er sich der Landschaftsphotographie und nimmt an der Nordwestküste Gebirgszüge wie die Cascades und Olympic Ranges auf. Als Bergsteiger begeistert er sich zudem für den »Hausberg« Seattles, den Mount Rainier.

1899
Curtis wird eingeladen, an der Alaska-Expedition des Eisenbahnmagnaten Harriman teilzunehmen. Er lernt auf dieser Reise bekannte Forscher kennen, die den Autodidakten in die Welt der Wissenschaften einführen und sein ethnologisches Interesse wecken.

1900
Curtis photographiert den Sonnentanz (»Sun Dance«) von Blood-, Blackfeet- und Algonquin-Indianern bei Browning, Montana. Er entwickelt den Plan, das Leben der Indianer photographisch zu dokumentieren, die mündlichen Überlieferungen der Stämme, ihre Legenden und Geschichten sowie

1892
Le photographe épouse Clara Phillips. Plusieurs membres des familles Curtis et Phillips collaborent, au cours des années suivantes, à l'entreprise photographique d'Edward.

1893
Curtis s'associe à l'atelier de Thomas Guptil.

1895/96
Le photographe fait ses premiers portraits d'Indiens sur le Puget Sound et dans la réserve de Tulahip, dans les environs de Seattle.

1897
Edward Curtis se met à son compte et se donne pour raison sociale «Edward S. Curtis, Photographer and Photoengraver», même s'il abandonne peu après la gravure. Curtis devient le premier photographe mondain de Seattle et jouit également d'un grand renom de portraitiste à l'échelon national. Il se consacre en outre à la photographie de paysage et des chaînes de montagnes de la côte nord-ouest, comme celles des Cascades ou de l'Olympic Ranges. Par ailleurs, il se passionne en tant qu'alpiniste pour le Mont Rainier, la «montagne maison» de Seattle.

1899
Curtis est invité à participer à l'expédition en Alaska organisée par le magnat des chemins de fer Harriman. Il fait au cours de ce voyage la connaissance de célèbres explorateurs qui initient l'autodidacte à l'univers des sciences et éveillent son intérêt pour l'ethnologie.

1900
Curtis photographie la Danse du Soleil («Sun Dance») des Indiens Blood, Blackfeet et Algonquin dans les environs de Browning, Montana. Il conçoit le projet de documenter la vie des Indiens par la

business. Curtis becomes Seattle's leading society photographer, also enjoying a nationwide reputation for his portraits. In addition, he devotes himself to landscape photography, taking shots of the mountains of the north-west coast, such as the Cascades and the Olympic Ranges. As a mountaineer, he delights also in Mount Rainier, a peak in Seattles's "own backyard".

1899
Curtis is invited to accompany the railway magnate Harriman on his expedition to Alaska. During the journey, he gets to know several prominent scientists, who introduce the autodidact to the world of science, awakening his interest in ethnology.

die Biographien der berühmtesten Häuptlinge und Krieger festzuhalten, Sprachstudien zu betreiben und Gesänge aufzuzeichnen, um sie später in Noten zu transkribieren.

1903
Für sein Forschungsprojekt, das den Titel *The North American Indian* trägt, sucht Curtis ab 1903 Geldgeber. Er hält zahlreiche Vorträge in den USA und besucht viele Indianerstämme.

1904
Curtis porträtiert den Präsidenten Theodore Roosevelt und gewinnt mit ihm einen prominenten Förderer seines Projektes.

photographie, de consigner les traditions orales des tribus, leurs légendes et leurs histoires, de fixer par écrit les biographies des chefs et des guerriers les plus célèbres, d'étudier leurs langues et d'enregistrer leurs chants pour les transcrire plus tard dans des partitions.

1903
A partir de 1903, Curtis recherche des bailleurs de fonds pour financer son projet de recherche, intitulé *The North American Indian*. Il fait de nombreuses conférences à travers les Etats-Unis et rend visite à un grand nombre de tribus indiennes.

1904
Curtis fait le portrait du président Theodore Roosevelt, en qui il gagne un éminent défenseur de son projet.

The Desert Queen, 1901
An example of Curtis' more exotic studio work
Die Königin der Wüste
Ein Beispiel für eine ausgefallenere Studioarbeit von Curtis
La Reine du Désert
Un exemple de travail de studio parmi les plus exotiques de Curtis

The Egyptian, 1901
A society portrait by Curtis which brought him considerable nationwide fame as a portrait photographer
Die Ägypterin
Ein Gesellschaftsporträt von Curtis, das ihm landesweiten Ruhm als Porträtphotograph einbrachte
L'Egyptienne
L'un des portraits mondains de Curtis qui lui valut quelque renom national en tant que portraitiste

THE SEATTLE SUNDAY TIMES. NOV. 3. 1912.

SOCIETY

"CURTIS INDIANS."

The latest fad among Seattle's daughters is posing in Indian costume at the Curtis Studio. No. 1 is Miss Dorothy Perry; No. 2, Miss Caroline Bruen; No. 3, Miss Katherine Brown; No. 4, Miss Mollie Killhour, and No. 5, Miss Ruth Boston.

Seattle society ladies dressed up as Indian squaws by Curtis in his studio. "The Seattle Sunday Times", 3 November 1912
Die Damen der Gesellschaft von Seattle wurden von Curtis in seinem Studio als indianische Squaws verkleidet. »The Seattle Sunday Times«, 3. November 1912
Dames de la société de Seattle habillées en squaws indiennes, photographiées par Curtis dans son studio. « The Seattle Sunday Times », 3 novembre 1912

An Indian profile, crossed arrows and a tipi. This design was embossed on the mounts of portraits done in Curtis' studio, undated, ca. 1910
Indianerprofil, gekreuzte Pfeile und ein Tipi. Dieser Prägestempel wurde für die auf Karton aufgezogenen Studioporträts verwendet, nicht datiert, ca. 1910
Indien de profil, flèches croisées et tipi, c'est le cachet en usage sur les supports cartonnés des portraits du Studio Curtis, non daté, vers 1910

1900
He conceives of the plan to photographically document Indian life, to record the tribes' oral tradition, their legends and stories, to note down the biographies of the most renowned chiefs and warriors, to study the Indian languages, and to record tribal songs with a view to transcribing them later into musical notation.

1906
Der New Yorker Großindustrielle, Finanzier und Philanthrop John Pierpont Morgan fördert Curtis' Buchprojekt.

1907
Der erste Band des *North American Indian* erscheint und wird von der Kritik gelobt. Die Ver-

1903

From this year on Curtis looks for funding for his project, which is entitled *The North American Indian*. He gives numerous lectures throughout the USA and visits many Indian tribes.

1904

Curtis takes a portrait of President Theodore Roosevelt, in the process gaining an important backer for his project.

1906

The New York industrialist, financier and philanthropist John Pierpont Morgan funds Curtis' book project.

Early portrait from the Curtis & Guptil studio, Seattle, ca. 1892
Frühe Porträtarbeit aus dem Curtis & Guptil-Studio, Seattle, ca. 1892
Portrait des débuts du Studio Curtis & Guptil, Seattle, vers 1892

Mrs S. E. S. Meany, ca. 1910
Portrait from Curtis' studio. The frame-like vignette is photographically printed and not three-dimensional
Mrs S. E. S. Meany, ca. 1910
Porträt aus dem Studio von Curtis. Die rahmenähnliche Vignette wurde wie ein Foto gedruckt und ist nicht dreidimensional
Mme S. E. S. Meany, vers 1910
Portrait du Studio Curtis. Le cadre avec ses bords estompés est imprimé par procédé photographique et n'est pas en trois dimensions

kaufszahlen bleiben jedoch niedrig. Curtis arbeitet trotz permanenter Finanzierungsschwierigkeiten und kriegsbedingter Unterbrechung bis 1930 weiter an dem Projekt. Unterstützt von einem Mitarbeiterteam besucht er zahlreiche Indianerstämme von der mexikanischen Grenze bis zum Bering-Meer und von der Pazifikküste bis zum Mississippi.

1906

Le grand industriel, financier et philanthrope new-yorkais John Pierpont Morgan soutient le projet de livre de Curtis.

1907

A sa parution, le premier volume de *North American Indian* est encensé par la critique. Le chiffre des ventes reste cependant peu élevé. Malgré des diffi-

Young lady with palms, 1920s
An example of Curtis' Los Angeles studio work. The photo is a framed "orotone" or goldtone print
Junge Dame mit Palme, 1920er
Ein Beispiel der Studioarbeit von Curtis in Los Angeles. Es handelt sich ein gerahmtes »Orotone«, das mittels Goldtönung erzielt wurde
Jeune dame aux palmier, années 1920
Un exemple du travail du Studio Curtis de Los Angeles. Il s'agit d'une épreuve obtenue par virage à l'or

Mount Rainier, ca. 1897
One of Curtis' lesser-known landscape photos,
subsequently printed as an "orotone"
Mount Rainier, ca. 1897
Eine eher unbekannte Landschaftsaufnahme,
die später als »Orotone« gedruckt wurde
Mount Rainier, vers 1897
Un des paysages mal connus de Curtis.
Le virage à l'or a été effectué ultérieurement

View from Heather Island. Harriman expedition to Alaska, 1898
Von Heather Island. Auf der Harriman-Expedition nach Alaska, 1898
Vue de Heather Island. Expédition Harriman en Alaska, 1898

1907

The first volume of *The North American Indian* appears. It meets with praise from the critics, but the sales figures remain low. Despite permanent financial difficulties and interruptions caused by war, Curtis continues his work on his project until 1930. Supported by a team of assistants, he visits numerous Indian tribes from the Mexican Border to the Bering Sea, and from the Pacific coast to the Mississippi.

1914

Curtis shoots *In the Land of the Headhunters*, a silent feature film about the Indians of the northwest coast. The film was later to act as a model for such ethnographically-minded feature film directors as Robert Flaherty.

1920

After his divorce, Curtis settles in Los Angeles and earns his living as a still photographer and cameraman for the Hollywood studios.

1928

After an eventful journey to the Arctic, Curtis concludes his researches for *The North American Indian*.

from 1930

The 20th and final volume of *The North American Indian* appears. Shortly afterwards, Curtis withdraws into private life, but for many years he continues working on a book with the working title *The Lure of Gold*. The book never appears.

1952

On 19 October Edward Sheriff Curtis dies in Los Angeles of a heart attack.

1914

Curtis dreht den Stummfilm *In the Land of the Headhunters* (Im Land der Kopfjäger) über die Indianer der Nordwestküste. Dieser Film sollte späteren ethnologisch orientierten Spielfilmregisseuren wie Robert Flaherty als Vorbild dienen.

1920

Nach seiner Scheidung läßt sich Curtis in Los Angeles nieder und finanziert seinen Lebensunterhalt als Standbildphotograph und Kameramann für die Hollywood Studios.

1928

Nach einer abenteuerlichen Arktisreise schließt Curtis die Recherchen für *The North American Indian* ab.

from 1930

Volume XX, der letzte Band von *The North American Indian* erscheint. Curtis zieht sich bald darauf ins Privatleben zurück, arbeitet jedoch noch viele Jahre an einem Buch mit dem Arbeitstitel *The Lure of Gold* (Der Lockruf des Goldes), das nie erscheinen sollte.

1952

Edward Sheriff Curtis stirbt am 19. Oktober nach einem Herzanfall in Los Angeles.

cultés financières permanentes et une interruption liée à la guerre, Curtis continue jusqu'en 1930 de travailler à son projet. Avec le soutien d'une équipe de collaborateurs, il rend visite aux nombreuses tribus indiennes qui vivent entre la frontière mexicaine et la mer de Béring, et entre la côte du Pacifique et le Mississippi.

1914

Curtis tourne le film muet *In the Land of the Headhunters* (Au pays des chasseurs de têtes) sur les Indiens de la côte nord-ouest. Ce film devait par la suite servir de modèle à des réalisateurs de films à orientation ethnologique comme Robert Flaherty.

1920

Après son divorce, Curtis s'installe à Los Angeles où il gagne sa vie comme opérateur et photographe de plateau pour les studios d'Hollywood.

1928

Après un voyage mouvementé dans l'Arctique, Curtis clôt ses recherches pour *The North American Indian*.

from 1930

Parution du XXe et dernier volume de *The North American Indian*. Curtis se retire peu de temps après pour se consacrer à sa vie privée, mais il travaille encore plusieurs années à un livre intitulé provisoirement *The Lure of Gold* (L'appel de l'or), et qui ne verra jamais le jour.

1952

Edward Sheriff Curtis meurt le 19 octobre à Los Angeles d'une crise cardiaque.

The Muir Glacier, seen from the west. Harriman expedition to Alaska, 1898
Der Muir-Gletscher von Westen aus gesehen. Auf der Harriman-Expedition nach Alaska, 1898
Le glacier Muir vu de l'Ouest. Expédition Harriman en Alaska, 1898

The way to the Nunatak – Ridged ice. Harriman expedition to Alaska, 1898
Der Weg zu den Nunatak – Vereister Höhenzug. Auf der Harriman-Expedition nach Alaska, 1898
Le chemin des Nunatak – Crêtes glacées. Expédition Harriman en Alaska, 1898

The Seattle Sunday Times.

A SEATTLE MAN'S TRIUMPH

Ed. Curtis makes photographs of secret rites of Navajoes — Scientists from Smithsonian Institution said this could not be done

MOORE THEATER

December 7 to 15 — Matinees Daily
The World Film Corporation
presents

In the Land of the Head Hunters

A Drama of Primitive Life on the Shores of the North Pacific
From Story Written and Picture Made by
EDWARD S. CURTIS

Every Participant an Indian and Every Incident True to Native Life.
Produced by the Seattle Film Co., Inc.
Interpretive Music Composed by John J. Braham from Phonographic Records of Indian Music.
Printing and Color Effects by Pierson Laboratories, Hochstetter Process.
Border Designs by Dugald Walker.
Cyclorama Stage Sets by Co-Operative Producing Company, executed by Frank Cambria.

SYNOPSIS

To gain power from the spirit forces, Motana, the son of a great chief, goes on a vigil journey. Through the fasting and hardship of the vigil he hopes to gain supernatural strength which will make him a chief not less powerful than his father, Kenada.

Article on Curtis' photographs of the Navaho Yebichai dance. "The Seattle Sunday Times", 23 May 1904
Artikel über die Aufnahmen, die Curtis beim Yebichaitanz der Navaho machte. »The Seattle Sunday Times«, 23. Mai 1904
Article consacré aux photographies de Curtis sur la danse des Navaho Yabachi. « The Seattle Sunday Times », 23 mai 1904

Programme for Curtis' silent film "In the Land of the Head Hunters", 1915
Programm für Curtis' Stummfilm »Im Land der Kopfjäger«, 1915
Programme du film muet de Curtis « Au pays des chasseurs de têtes », 1915

Motana, the hero of Curtis' silent film
"In the Land of the Head Hunters", 1914
Motana, Titelheld von Curtis' Stummfilm
»Im Land der Kopfjäger«, 1914
Motana, le héros du film de Curtis « Au pays
des chasseurs de têtes », 1914

Naida, the Proud Princess of Curtis' film
"In the Land of the Head Hunters", 1914
Naida, die stolze Prinzessin in Curtis' Film
»Im Land der Kopfjäger«, 1914
Naida, la fière princesse du film de Curtis
« Au pays des chasseurs de têtes », 1914

Tarzan, still photo, ca. 1921
Tarzan, Standbild, ca. 1921
Tarzan, photo du film, vers 1921

Ramses, still photo from "The Ten
Commandments", 1923
Ramses, Standbild aus dem Film
»Die zehn Gebote«, 1923
Ramsès, photo du film «Les Dix
Commandements», 1923

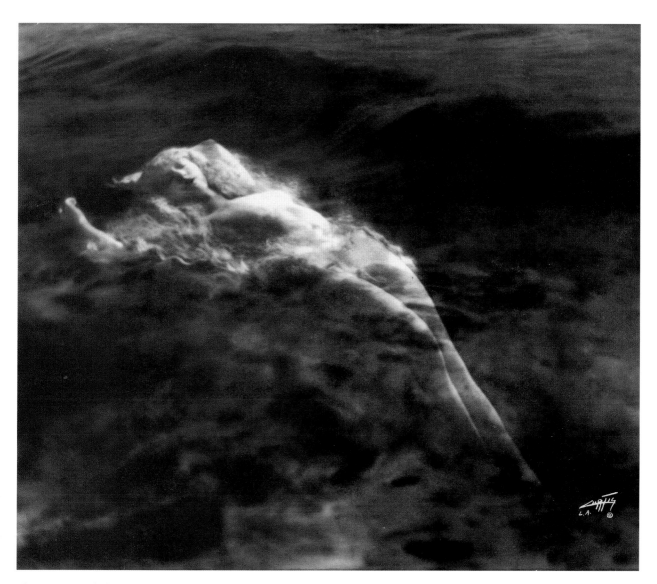

This interpretation of a foam-born Aphrodite,
possibly done in Hollywood in the early 30s,
is one of Curtis' late photographic works
Dieses Bild einer schaumgeborenen Aphrodite gehört
zu Curtis' späten Arbeiten und ist möglicherweise in
Hollywood Anfang der 30er Jahre entstanden
Cette interprétation d'une Aphrodite née de l'écume,
dont il se peut qu'elle ait été créée à Hollywood dans
les années 30, est l'une des dernières œuvres photo-
graphiques de Curtis

Bibliography
Bibliographie
Bibliographie

Books by Edward S. Curtis
Bücher von Edward S. Curtis
Livres d'Edward S. Curtis

Indian Days of the Long Ago
by Edward Sheriff Curtis. Illustrated with photographs by the author and drawings by F. N. Wilson. Yonkers-on-Hudson (NY): World Book Co., 1914; Reprint Berkeley (CA): Ten Speed/Tamarack Press, 1975 (Indian Life and Indian Lore).

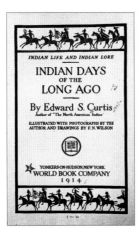

In the Land of the Head Hunters
by Edward Sheriff Curtis. Illustrated with photographs by the author. Yonkers-on-Hudson: World Book Co., 1915; Reprint: Berkeley (CA): Ten Speed/Tamarack Press, 1975 (Indian Life and Indian Lore).

"The Land of the Head Hunters"
Still photo | Standbild | Photo du film

The North American Indian
by Edward Sheriff Curtis. 20 vols.; vols. I–V, Cambridge (MA): The University Press; vols. VI–XX, Norwood (MA): The Plimpton Press, 1907–1930.

234

Books on Edward S. Curtis
Bücher über Edward S. Curtis
Livres sur Edward S. Curtis

Boesen, Victor, and Florence Curtis Graybill:
*Edward S. Curtis: Photographer of the North
American Indian.* New York: Dodd, Mead & Co.,
1977.

Cardozo, Christopher:
*Native Nations: First Americans as seen by Edward
S. Curtis.* Boston (MA): Bullfinch Press, 1993.

Coleman, A.D., and T.C. Mc Luhan:
*Curtis: His work. Introduction to Portraits from the
North American Indian by Edward S. Curtis.* New
York: Dutton, 1972.

Coleman, A.D.:
"Edward S. Curtis. The photographer as ethnolo-
gist." In: Coleman, A.D.: *Depth of Field. Essays
on Photography, Mass Media, and Lens Culture.*
Albuquerque (NM): University of New Mexico
Press, 1998.

Curtis, Edward Sheriff:
*In a Sacred Manner We Live: Photographs of the
North American Indian by Edward Sheriff Curtis.*
Barre (MA): Weathervane Books, 1972.

Curtis, Edward Sheriff:
*The North American Indians. Photographs by
Edward S. Curtis.* Text compiled with an introduction by Joseph Epes Brown. Millerton (NY): Aper-
ture, 1972.

Davis, Barbara A.:
*Edward S. Curtis: The Life and Times of a Shadow
Catcher.* San Francisco (CA): Chronicle Books,
1985.

Gidley, Mick:
*The Vanishing Race: Selections from Edward S.
Curtis' The North American Indian.* New York:
Taplinger Publishing, 1977.

Gidley, Mick:
"From the Hopi Snake Dance to 'The Ten Commandments'. Edward S. Curtis as film-maker." In:
Studies in Visual Communication, Summer 1982,
pp. 70–79.

Gidley, Mick:
*Edward S. Curtis and The North American
Indian, Incorporated.* New York & Cambridge:
Cambridge University Press, 1998.

Graybill, Florence Curtis, and Victor Boesen:
*Edward Sheriff Curtis – Visions of a Vanishing
Race.* New York: Thomas Y. Crowell, 1976.

Goetzmann, William N.:
"The arcadian landscapes of Edward S. Curtis." In:
Castleberry, May: *Perpetual Mirage. Photographic
Narratives of the Desert West.* New York: Whitney
Museum/Harry N. Abrams, 1996, pp. 83–91.

Hartmann, Sadakichi:
"E.S. Curtis, photo-historian." In: *The Valiant
Knights of Daguerre.* Berkeley (CA): University
of California Press, 1978, pp. 262–272.

Hausman, Gerald, and Bob Kapoun:
*Prayer to the Great Mystery. The Uncollected
Writings and Photography of Edward S. Curtis.*
New York: St. Martin's Press, 1995.

Kate, Herman F.C. ten:
The North American Indian. Amsterdam: Kon-
inglijk Nederlands Aarrijkskundig Genootschap,
1910.

Lowry, Shannon:
*Natives of the Far North. Alaska's Vanishing
Culture in the Eye of Edward Sheriff Curtis.*
Mechanicsburg (PA): Stackpole Books, 1994.

Lyman, Christopher M.:
*The Vanishing Race and Other Illusions: Pho-
tographs by Edward S. Curtis.* New York: Pan-
theon Books, in association with the Smithsonian
Press, 1982.

Pritzker, Barry:
Edward S. Curtis. New York: Crescent Books,
1993.

Rice, Leland:
Edward S. Curtis: The Kwakiutl, 1910–1914.
Irvine (CA): University of California Press, 1976.

General literature
Allgemeine Literatur
Ouvrages généraux

Alison, Jane (ed.) et al.:
Native Nations. Journeys in American Photography.
London: Barbican Art Gallery, 1998.

Catlin, George:
Letters and Notes on the North American Indian.
Edited and with an introduction by Michael M.
Mooney. New York: Gramercy Books, 1975.

Edmonds, Margot, and Ella E. Clark:
Voices of the Winds. Native American Legends.
New York: Facts on File, 1989.

Fleming, Paula Richardson, and Judith Lynn
Luskey:
The North American Indians in Early Photographs.
New York: Dorset Press, 1986.

Fleming, Paula Richardson, and Judith Lynn
Luskey:
*Schattenfänger. Die Indianer Nordamerikas in
historischen Meisterphotographien.* Munich: Beck,
1993

Groneveld, Anneke et al.:
*Odagot. Indianen gefotografeerd 1860–1920. Pho-
tographs of American Indians 1860–1920.* Amster-
dam/Rotterdam: Fragment Uitgeverij/Museum
voor Volkenkunde, 1992. (Fotografie uit de collec-
tie van het Museum voor Volkenkunde, 6).

Josephy, Alvin M.:
*500 nations. An illustrated History of North Ame-
rican Indians.* New York: Alfred A. Knopf, 1994.

Penney, David W.; Lisa A. Roberts, and Nancy
Barr:
*Images of Identity. American Indians in Photo-
graphs.* Detroit: The Detroit Institute of Arts,
1994.

Schwarz, Angelo:
*Cronaca fotografica del genocido delle nazioni
indiane d'America.* Ivrea: Priuli & Verlucca, 1980.

Curtis encampment, Idaho

Photographic credits
Bildnachweis
Crédits photographiques

The publishers wish to thank the institutions named below for their cooperation and for granting permission to reproduce works in this book. Most of the images derive from Curtis' encyclopaedic work *The North American Indian*, 1907–1930 (abbreviated to: NAI). All the illustrations from NAI have been reproduced from the complete set of NAI (designated set number 8) in the possession of the Niedersächsischen Staats- und Universitätsbibliothek, Abteilung für Handschriften und seltene Drucke [Lower Saxony State and University Library, Manuscript and Rare Print Department], in Göttingen, and bearing the catalogue number: H. Amer. II, 12, 1–20.

In the 20 textual volumes of NAI, the gravure illustrations have no page or plate numbers. The photos reproduced from NAI are identified by giving the NAI vol. nr. followed by the page nr. nearest to the gravure print, abbreviated, e. g., as follows: vol. X, p. 56.

The 20 textual volumes of NAI are accompanied by 20 portfolios of gravure-printed photographs. Here, photos reproduced from the portfolios (abbreviated to: folio) are identified by giving the relevant volume and plate number, e. g.: NAI folio X, pl. 356.

Photos reproduced from material held by the Department of Prints and Photographs of the Library of Congress, Washington DC, (abbreviated to: LC), are identified with LC and the relevant negative number.

Photos reproduced from material held by the University of Washington Libraries, Seattle, WA, (abbreviated to: UW), are likewise identified by their respective negative number.

Picture material has also kindly been supplied by the Seattle gallery Flury and Company (abbreviated to: Flury), which specializes in Curtis photographs.

Der Verlag dankt den im folgenden genannten Institutionen für die Zusammenarbeit und für die Erteilung der Reproduktionsrechte.

Die meisten Abbildungen im vorliegenden Buch stammen aus Curtis' Werk *The North American Indian*, 1907–1930 (abgekürzt NAI). Als Reproduktionsvorlage diente die mit Nr. 8 bezeichnete vollständige Ausgabe des Titels, die sich im Besitz der Niedersächsischen Staats- und Universitätsbibliothek, Abteilung für Handschriften und seltene Drucke in Göttingen befindet und die Signatur »H. Amer. II, 12, 1–20« trägt. Die Abbildungen in den 20 Textbänden der NAI sind weder durch Seitenzahlen noch durch Abbildungsnummern gekennzeichnet. Im Abbildungsverzeichnis ist die Seitenzahl angegeben, die der Abbildung am nächsten steht, abgekürzt z. B.: vol. X, p. 56.

Für die 20 Portfolios (abgekürzt folio) der NAI mit Photogravüren erfolgt die Bezeichnung der Abbildung nach Bandzahl und Nummer der Bildtafel (pl. für plate), abgekürzt z. B.: NAI folio X, pl. 356.

Die Bildvorlagen vom Department of Prints and Photographs of the Library of Congress, Washington, DC, (Abkürzung: LC) sind mit der Nummer des Negativs aufgeführt.

Das Abbildungsmaterial der University of Washington Libraries in Seattle (abgekürzt UW) ist ebenfalls mit der Negativnummer verzeichnet.

Die auf Curtis- Photographien spezialisierte Galerie Flury and Company in Seattle (abgekürzt: Flury) stellte ebenfalls Bildmaterial zur Verfügung.

L'éditeur remercie de leur collaboration les institutions suivantes, qui ont également bien voulu lui accorder les autorisations de reproduction nécessaires à cet ouvrage.

La plupart des illustrations proviennent de l'œuvre de Curtis *The North American Indian*, 1907–1930 (en abrégé NAI.). Les reproductions figurant dans le présent volume ont été réalisées à partir de l'édition complète, répertoriée sous le n° 8, qui se trouve en possession de la Niedersächsische Staats- und Universitätsbibliothek de Göttingen, où elle est conservée au département des manuscrits et des imprimés rares et précieux sous la cote « H. Amer. II, 12, 1–20 ». Les planches des 20 volumes des NAI. ne font l'objet d'aucune pagination, que ce soit sous la forme de numéros de page ou d'illustration. Le numéro de page qui figure dans la table des illustrations est celui de la page la plus proche de l'illustration en question, soit par exemple : vol. X, p. 56.

En ce qui concerne les 20 portfolios (en abrégé folio) de photogravures qui accompagnent les volumes des NAI., ce sont les numéros du volume et de la planche (pl. pour planche) qui servent à identifier les illustrations, soit par exemple: NAI folio X, pl. 356.

Les documents photographiques du département des imprimés et des photographies de la Library of Congress de Washington DC (en abrégé LC) sont mentionnés par le numéro du négatif.

Le matériau photographique en provenance de l'University of Washington Libraries de Seattle (en abrégé UW) est lui aussi désigné par le numéro du négatif.

L'éditeur remercie également la Galerie Flury and Company de Seattle (en abrégé Flury), spécialisée dans l'œuvre de Curtis, qui a bien voulu mettre des photographies à sa disposition.

l. = left | links | à gauche
r. = right | rechts | à droite
t. = top | oben | ci-dessus
c. = centre | Mitte
b. = bottom | unten | ci-dessous

Page | Seite:

2 UW 2807; 5 LC-USZ62-116676 (also NAI folio I, pl. 28); 8 LC-USZ62-57487; 9 LC-USZ62-112209; 10 LC-USZ62-109702; 11 Flury; 12 NAI folio VI, pl. 196; 15 NAI folio VI, pl. 213; 16 NAI folio IV, pl. 120; 17 NAI folio V, pl. 153; 18 NAI folio XVIII, pl. 640; 19 NAI folio XIV, pl. 472; 20 NAI folio V, pl. 180; 23 NAI folio I, pl. 21; 61 Flury (goldtone same as gravure in NAI folio I, pl. 1); 32 NAI vol. I, p. 52; 39 NAI vol. I, p. 64; 44 NAI vol. I, p. 52; 51 NAI folio I, pl. 14; 62 Flury (goldtone same as NAI folio I, pl. 20); 63 NAI folio I, pl. 32; 64 NAI folio I, pl. 15; 65 NAI folio VIII, pl. 266; 66 NAI vol. I, p. 66; 67 NAI folio I, pl. 34; 69 t. LC-USZ62-48378; 69 b. NAI vol. I, p. 116; 70 NAI vol. I, p. 36; 71 NAI folio III, pl. 76; 72 NAI vol. I, p. 136; 73 NAI vol. I, p. 110; 74 l. NAI vol. I, p. 94; 74 r. NAI vol. I, p. 102; 75 l. NAI vol. I, p. 140; 75 r. NAI vol. I, p. 138; 77 NAI folio XVIII, pl. 633; 78 LC-USZ62-83601 (also NAI folio II, pl. 56); 79 LC-USZ62-52477; 80 LC-USZ62-105385 (also NAI folio XIII, pl. 451); 81 NAI folio XIII, pl. 445; 83 NAI folio II, pl. 61; 84 NAI vol. II, p. 32; 85 NAI folio II, pl. 49; 86 LC-USZ62-101172; 87 LC-USZ62-47851; 89 l. LC-USZ62-113094; 89 b. NAI vol. III, p. 96; 90 NAI vol. IV, p. 116; 91 LC-USZ62-46970 (also NAI folio IV, pl. 127); 93 NAI folio III, p. 108; 94 NAI folio IV, pl. 125; 95 NAI folio III, pl. 85; 97 t. NAI vol. VI, p. 18; 97 b LC-USZ62-66699; 98 NAI folio I, pl. 21; 99 NAI folio III, pl. 104; 100 NAI vol. IV, p. 78; 101 Flury

(goldtone print s. also NAI vol. IV, frontispiece); 102 NAI vol. IV, p. 166; 103 NAI vol. IV, p. 150; 104 NAI vol. IV, p.74; 105 NAI vol. IV, p.136; 106 Flury (goldtone print, also NAI folio III, pl. 80); 107 NAI folio III, pl. 111; 108 NAI folio V, pl. 150; 109 NAI vol. V, p. 74; 110 LC-USZ62-46967; 111 LC-USZ62-106995 (also NAI folio XVIII, pl. 625); 112 NAI vol. XVIII, p. 170; 113 NAI vol. XIX, p. 78; 114 LC-USZ62-105387 (also NAI folio VIII, pl. 281); 115 LC-USZ62-105382; 116 LC-USZ 62-112273; 117 NAI vol. IV, p. 28; 118 NAI folio IV, pl. 142; 119 NAI vol. VIII, p. 4; 120 NAI folio IV, pl. 128; 121 NAI folio XIX, pl. 669; 122 NAI folio VI, pl. 199; 123 NAI folio IV, pl. 133; 124 NAI folio III, pl. 82; 125 NAI folio VI, pl. 200; 126 LC-USZ62-101185 (also NAI vol. V, p. 86); 127 LC-USZ62-83965 (also NAI vol. V, pl. 163, cropped); 128 NAI folio VII, pl. 255; 129 NAI folio VII, pl. 234; 130 NAI vol. VII, p. 46; 131 NAI folio XIII, p. 470; 132 LC-USZ62-79772; 133 NAI folio XVIII, pl. 634; 134 NAI folio VI, pl. 215; 135 NAI folio VII, pl. 242; 136 LC-USZ61-2088 (also NAI vol. VIII, p. 24); 137 NAI folio VIII, pl. 256; 138 NAI vol. VII, p. 68; 139 LC-USZ62-98071 (also NAI folio VII, pl. 235); 140 NAI folio XIV, pl. 489; 141 NAI folio XIV, pl. 501; 143 NAI folio XII, pl. 405; 144 l. NAI folio XII, pl. 415; 144 r. NAI folio XII, pl. 414; 145 LC-USZ62-88309; 146 NAI folio XII, pl. 413; 147 Flury (also LC-USZ 62-102040); 148 t. LC-USZ62-112224; 148 b. LC-USZ 62-112226; 149 t. LC-USZ62-97088; 149 b. LC-USZ 62-48379; 151 NAI vol. XII, p. 136; 152 NAI folio XII, pl. 404; 153 LC-USZ63-85415 (also NAI vol. XII, p. 142); 154 LC-USZ62-97071; 155 NAI vol. XII, p. 156; 156 NAI folio XII, pl. 424; 157 LC-USZ62-83960 (also NAI folio XVII, pl. 608); 158 NAI vol. XVI, p. 80; 159 NAI folio XVI, pl. 544; 160 NAI folio XVI, pl. 571; 161 NAI folio XVI, pl. 573; 162 NAI folio XVI, pl. 578; 163 NAI vol. XVI, p. 44;

164 LC-USZ62-112230; 165 LCUSZ62-112223; 166 NAI folio XVI, pl. 564; 167 NAI folio XVI, pl. 565; 168 NAI folio XVI, pl. 570; 169 NAI folio XVI, pl. 567; 170 LC-USZ62-115816 (also NAI vol. XVII, p. 56); 171 NAI vol. XVII, p. 52; 172 NAI folio XVII, pl. 592; 173 NAI vol. XVII, p. 54; 175 LC-USZ62-90801 (also NAI folio XI, pl. 365); 177 NAI folio IX, pl. 326; 178 LC-USZ62-101261 (also NAI vol. XIII, p. 28); 179 LC-USZ62-110506 (also NAI folio XIII, pl. 436); 180 NAI folio IX, pl. 304; 181 NAI folio IX, pl. 299; 182 NAI vol. X, p. 90; 183 NAI folio IX, pl. 303; 184 NAI folio VIII, pl. 284; 185 NAI folio VIII, pl. 274; 186 NAI folio XI, pl. 376; 187 NAI vol. XI, p. 58; 188 NAI vol. XI, p. 54; 189 NAI folio XI, pl. 382; 190 t. NAI folio XI, pl. 396; 190 b. NAI vol. XI, p. 76; 191 NAI folio XI, pl. 395; 193 Flury; 194 NAI folio X, pl. 358; 195 LC-USZ62-52200 (also NAI folio X, pl. 337); 196 NAI vol. X, p. 162; 197 NAI folio X, pl. 348; 198 l. NAI vol. X, p. 203; 198 r. NAI vol. X, p. 248; 199 l. NAI vol. X, p. 230; 199 r. NAI vol. X, p. 228; 200 NAI vol. X, p. 176; 201 NAI vol. X, p. 232; 202 NAI vol. X, p. 242; 203 NAI vol. X, p. 194; 204 Flury (also LCUSZ62-101256); 205 Flury (also LCUSZ62-96724); 206 NAI folio X, pl. 343; 207 NAI folio XI, pl. 397; 208 NAI vol. XI, frontispiece; 209 LC-USZ62-110505 (also NAI folio IX, pl. 300); 210 NAI folio X, pl. 329; 211 NAI folio X, pl. 334; 213 NAI folio XX, pl. 694; 214 NAI vol. XX, p. 80; 215 NAI vol. XX, p. 54; 216 NAI folio XX, pl. 716; 217 LCUSZ62-107281 (also NAI vol. XX, p. 204); 218 l. UW 2805; 219 LC-USZ62-66633; 218 Flury; 221 b. l. UW 147; 221 b. r. UW 152; 220 t. Flury; 222 t. Flury; 222 b. UW; 223 b. l. UW; 223 t. c. UW; 223 b. r. Flury; 224 Flury; 225 UW 98; 226 UW 28; 227 UW 100; 228 l. UW; 229 c. r. Flury; 229 c. l. Flury; 228 r. UW 18441; 230 t. l. Flury; 230 b. r. Flury; 231 Flury; 232 b. r. UW; 235 Flury

Notes

1] Quoted from Victor Boesen and Florence Curtis Graybill: *Edward S. Curtis: Photographer of the North American Indian*. New York: Dodd, Mead & Co., New York, 1977, p. 186.

2] The idea of reducing photographic portraits to calling card size (6 x 9 cm) was patented in 1851 by the photographer André Adolphe-Eugène Disdéri (1819–1889). The small portraits soon became highly popular. People made presents of their own portraits to their relatives, but also began to collect photographs of prominent people.

3] On an invoice dated 1 October 1918, Curtis is named as the "Proprietor and manager". (Invoice, University of Washington, Special Collection Library, Sign. 484/2/8.)

4] On the wrapper of the postcards is printed: "Curtis Copyrighted Photo Tint Indian Postal Cards, Published by E. S. Curtis, Seattle, Washington."

5] One such invitation card that has survived bears the text: "Edward Curtis and his Indians. A picture talk, with Stereopticon, Christensen's Hall, Arcade Building, Monday, No. 13, at 8.15 p.m. Tickets, $ 1. For sale at Curtis' Gallery, at The [Seattle] Times, and at the door."

6] George Bird Grinnell in *Scribner's Magazine*, quoted from Boesen and Graybill (1977), p. 48.

7] Ralph W. Andrews, "He knew the Red Man: Edward S. Curtis, photographer", in *The Magazine of Western History*, Montana (Helena, MA). vol. 14, no. 2, April 1964, pp. 2–13.

8] Cf. Paula Richardson Fleming, and Judith Lynn Luskey, *The North American Indians in Early Photographs*, New York: Dorset Press, 1986.

9] Quoted from Boesen and Graybill 1977, p. 35

10] The shots he took during this period were later printed in Roosevelt's autobiography. A portrait of the president that he did at Sagamore Hill Curtis himself described without any trace of false modesty: "My picture of the President is great. It is quite different from anything before taken and, I believe, will be considered by all who know him, a splendid likeness. I made no effort to retouch the face and make him a smooth-visaged individual without a line or anything to show his character … Background, clothing and everything is carried in one great mass of shadow, bringing out the face, with its great strength of character, as the only thing that we see, and I believe it is good." Quoted from Mick Gidley, *Edward S. Curtis and the North American Indian, Incorporated*, New York & Cambridge: Cambridge University Press, 1998, p. 62.

11] C. T. Conover, "The monumental work of Edward S. Curtis," in *The Seattle Times*, Sunday, 21 June 1953, pp. 4–5.

12] C. T. Conover, "The monumental work of Edward S. Curtis," in *The Seattle Times*, Sunday, 21 June 1953, pp. 4–5.

13] *The Seattle Times*, 15 November 1903.

14] *Potlatches* are Indian ceremonial feasts marked by the host's lavish distribution of gifts requiring some return in kind. The word potlatch comes from the Chinook and means "to give."

15] Curtis, *The North American Indian*, vol. XX, 1930, p. xvii

16] Thus, for example, the collection of 100 first-rate prints that are currently in the keeping of the New York Public Library, which in all likelihood came from Morgan's holdings.

17] The archiving and labelling of the exposures was conducted with great care at the Curtis Studio. In some cases the negative numbers were altered, for on some prints it can be seen that the numbers have been replaced by new ones.

18] Given the large degree of manual work involved, it is not surprising that volumes and portfolios I–XI, which were produced by the renowned firm John Andrew and Son in Boston, differ significantly from volumes XII–XX. The latter were produced by Suffolk Engraving and Electrotyping Co., a firm also located in Boston, but which operated to less exacting standards. The difference in the illustrations from the two firms is visible not least in their tone; from volume XII onwards they have more of a light brown tinge. The colour saturation also seems to be weaker in the later volumes, which is to say the black tones are less opaque.

19] Undated Curtis Studio sales catalogue, published around 1907 and printed several times in a slightly amended edition to ca 1918 (measurements in inches): prints "Small, from 6 1/2 x 8 1/2 plates, $ 3.00; intermediate, from 14 x 17 plates, $ 15,00; large, from 18 x 22 plates, $ 20.00." No mention is made of whether these are photogravures or silver gelatin prints, although the latter is more likely. There is a note about the frames: "Exclusive frames especially designed and toned to harmonize with the Indian studies can be purchased at prices ranging from $ 2.50 each up."

20] Curtis specifies the prices for the 'Curt-tones' as follows (measurements in inches): "8 x 10, framed, $ 10.00; 11 x 14, framed, $ 15.00; 14 x 17, framed, $ 30.00; 18 x 22, framed, $ 50.00. No Curt-tones sold unframed. Crating and packing shipments $ 1.00."

21] George Catlin, *Letters and Notes on the North American Indians*, edited and with an introduction by Michael M. Mooney, New York: Gramercy Books 1975. First edition: London, 1841.

22] Ibidem, p. 1.

23] Undated article [reprint], *Oregonian*, undated reprint. University of Washington, Special Collection Library, Sign. 484/2/8.

24] "The book represents an outlay of a million and a half dollars." Announcement by Charles Rice, Curtis' tour manager, for a lecture by the photographer in New York (in connection with the musicale by Henry F. Gilbert). Cf. University of Washington, Special Collection Library, Sign. N 970.1 C94w.

25] Anonymous, "A Seattle Man's Triumph," *The Seattle Sunday Times*, magazine section, 22 May 1904, p. 2.

26] Ralph W. Andrews, "He knew the Red Man: Edward S. Curtis, photographer," in *The Magazine of Western History*, Montana (Helena, MA), vol. 14, no. 2, April 1964, p. 5.

27] Letter from Matilda Cox Stevenson, Smithsonian Institution, Bureau of American Ethnology, Washington, D.C., 15 March 1905.

28] Curtis, *The North American Indian, vol. IV*, 1909, p. 4.

Anmerkungen

1] Zitiert nach: Victor Boesen und Florence Curtis Graybill: *Edward S. Curtis: Photographer of the North American Indian*. New York: Dodd, Mead & Co., 1977, S. 186.

2] Die Idee, Photoporträts auf das Visitenkartenformat 6 x 9 cm zu verkleinern, ließ sich 1851 der Photograph Adolph-Eugène Disdéri (1819–1889) patentieren. Die kleinen Porträts erfreuten sich bald großer Beliebtheit. Man verschenkte die eigene Aufnahme in der Verwandtschaft, begann aber auch, Aufnahmen von Prominenten zu sammeln.

3] Auf einer Rechnung von 1918 wird Curtis als »Besitzer und Geschäftsführer« bezeichnet. Rechnung vom 1. Oktober 1918, University of Washington, Special Collection Library, Sign. 484/2/8.

4] Auf dem Verpackungsumschlag der Postkarten steht: »Curtis Copyrighted Photo Tint Indian Postal Cards, Published by E. S. Curtis, Seattle, Washington.«

5] Eine erhaltene Einladungskarte trägt den Text: »Edward Curtis and his Indians. A picture talk, with Stereopticon, Christensen's Hall, Arcade Building, Monday, No. 13 at. 8.15 p.m. Tickets, $ 1. For sale at Curtis' Gallery, at The [Seattle] Times, and at the door.«

6] George Bird Grinnell in *Scribner's Magazine*, zitiert nach: Boesen und Graybill 1977, S. 48.

7] Ralph W. Andrews: »He knew the Red Man: Edward S. Curtis, photographer.« In: *The Magazine of Western History*, Montana (Helena, MA), Vol. 14, No. 2, April 1964, S. 2–13.

8] Vgl. Paula Richardson Fleming und Judith Lynn Luskey: *Schattenfänger. Die Indianer Nordamerikas in historischen Meisterphotographien*. München: Beck 1996, 3. Aufl., S. 111 f.

9] Zitiert nach Boesen und Graybill 1977, S. 35.

10] Die Aufnahmen, die in diesem Zeitraum entstanden, wurden später in Roosevelts Autobiographie abgedruckt. Ein Porträt des Präsidenten, das in Sagamore Hill entstand, bezeichnete Curtis selbst ohne falsche Bescheidenheit als großartig. Er schreibt: »Es ist so ganz anders als die bisherigen Aufnahmen von ihm, und alle, die ihn kennen, werden ihn meiner Ansicht nach außergewöhnlich gut getroffen finden. Ich habe auf Retuschen verzichtet, denn ich wollte nicht einen Mann mit glattem Gesicht ohne Falten und andere charakteristische Züge aus ihm machen. (...) Der Hintergrund, die Kleidung und alles andere sind von einem einzigen großen Schatten bedeckt, um das Gesicht mit der für ihn typischen Strenge herauszubringen; es ist das einzige, was wir sehen. Ich glaube, das Bild ist gut.« Zitiert nach: Gidley 1998, S. 62.

11] C. T. Conover: »The monumental work of Edward S. Curtis.« In: *The Seattle Times*, Sonntag, 21. Juni 1953, S. 4–5.

12] Vgl. C. T. Conover: »The monumental work of Edward S. Curtis.« In: *The Seattle Times*, Sonntag, 21. Juni 1953, S. 4–5.

13] *The Seattle Times*, 15. November 1903.

14] Das Wort *potlach* stammt aus der Chinock-Sprache und bedeutet »geben«.

15] Curtis, *The North American Indian*, Vol. XX, 1930, S. XVII.

16] So zum Beispiel eine Sammlung von 100 exzellen-

ten Abzügen, die heute in der New Yorker Public Library aufbewahrt wird und möglicherweise aus den Beständen von Pierpont Morgan stammt.

17] Die Archivierung und Kennzeichnung der Aufnahmen wurde im Studio Curtis mit Sorgfalt durchgeführt. In einigen Fällen wurden Negativnummern verändert, denn auf einigen Abzügen ist erkennbar, daß die Nummern ausgekratzt und durch neue ersetzt wurden.

18] Bei so viel Handarbeit ist es nicht verwunderlich, daß sich die Bände und Mappen I bis XI, die von der renommierten Firma John Andrew and Son in Boston produziert wurden, von den Bänden XII bis XX deutlich unterscheiden. Für letztere zeichnet das ebenfalls in Boston arbeitende und etwas weniger perfekte Unternehmen Suffolk Engraving and Electrotyping Co. verantwortlich. Die Abbildungen haben in den Bänden eine unterschiedliche Qualität, etwa in der Druckfarbe; sie zeigen ab Band XII ein eher helles Braun. Die Farbsättigung scheint ebenfalls weniger stark zu sein, d.h. die Schwärzen sind weniger deckend.

19] Undatierter Verkaufskatalog des Curtis-Studios, erschienen um 1907, in leicht veränderter Ausgabe mehrfach aufgelegt, mit Maßen in Inch: Prints »Small, from 6 1/2 x 8 1/2 plates, $ 3.00; Intermediate, from 14 x 17 plates, $ 15.00; Large, from 18 x 22 plates, $ 20.00.« Es ist nicht erwähnt, ob es sich um Gravüren oder um Silbergelatine-Abzüge handelt; letzteres ist aber wahrscheinlich. Seit 1909 enthält der Katalog einen Text zu den Bilderrahmen: »Exclusive frames especially designed and toned to harmonize with the Indian studies can be purchased at prizes ranging from $ 2.50 each up.«

20] Hierfür gibt Curtis die folgenden Preise an: »8 x 10, framed, $ 10.00; 11 x 14, framed, $ 15.00; 14 x 17, framed, $ 30.00; 18 x 22, framed, $ 50.00. No Curt-tònes sold unframed. Crating and packing shipments $ 1.00.«

21] George Catlin: Letters and Notes on the North American Indians. Hrsg. von Michael M. Mooney. New York: Gramercy Books 1975. Erstausgabe London 1841.

22] Ibidem, S. 1.

23] Gedruckte Seite unbekannter Quelle, aus: Oregonian, undatierter Nachdruck. University of Washington, Special Collection Library, Sign. 484/2/8.

24] »The book represents an outlay of a million and a half dollars.« Ankündigung eines Vortrages von Curtis durch Charles Rice, dem Manager von Entertainment Tour, New York (in Verbindung mit Henry F. Gilberts Musical). Vgl. University of Washington, Special Collection Library, Sign. N 970.1 C94w.

25] Anonymus: »A Seattle Man's Triumph«. In: The Seattle Sunday Times, magazine section, 22. Mai 1904, S. 2.

26] Ralph W. Andrews: »He knew the Red Man: Edward S. Curtis, photographer.« In: The Magazine of Western History, Montana (Helena, MA), Vol. 14, No. 2, April 1964, S. 5.

27] Brief von Matilda Cox Stevenson, Smithsonian Institution, Bureau of American Ethnology, Washington, D.C., 15. März 1905.

28] Curtis, The North American Indian, Vol. IV, 1909, S. 4.

Notes

1] Cit. d'après Victor Boesen et Florence Curtis Graybill: Edward S. Curtis: Photographer of the North American Indian. New York: Dodd, Mead & Co., 1977, p. 186.

2] L'idée de réaliser des portraits photographiques au format réduit 6 x 9 cm des cartes de visite est à l'origine celle du photographe Adolphe-Eugène Disdéri (1819–1889), qui la fit breveter en 1851. Ces petits portraits jouirent rapidement d'une grande popularité. Si on offrait alors volontiers sa propre photo aux gens de sa famille, on commença aussi à collectionner des photos de célébrités.

3] Une facture du 1er octobre 1918 désigne Curtis comme «propriétaire et directeur». University of Washington, Special Collection Library, Sign. 484/2/8.

4] On peut lire sur l'enveloppe qui servait d'emballage à ces cartes postales: «Curtis Copyrighted Photo Tint Indian Postal Cards, Published by E. S. Curtis, Seattle, Washington.»

5] Une carte d'invitation nous est parvenue qui porte le texte suivant: «Edward Curtis and his Indians. A picture talk, with Stereopticon, Christensen's Hall, Arcade Building, Monday, No. 13 at 8. 15 p. m. Tickets, $ 1. For sale at Curtis' Gallery, at The [Seattle] Times and at the door.»

6] George Bird Grinnell dans Scribner's Magazine, cit. d'après Boesen et Graybill 1977, p. 48.

7] Ralph W. Andrews: «He knew the Red Man: Edward S. Curtis, photographer», dans The magazine of Western history, Montana (Helena, MA), vol. 14, n° 2, avril 1964, p. 2–13.

8] Cf. Paula Richardson Fleming et Judith Lynn Luskey: The North American Indians in early photographs. New York: Dorset Press, 1986. Munich: Beck 1996, 3e éd., p. 111 sq.

9] Cit. d'après Boesen et Graybill 1977, p. 35.

10] Les clichés qui datent de cette période furent reproduits par la suite dans l'autobiographie de Roosevelt. Curtis lui-même qualifia sans fausse modestie de superbe un portrait qu'il avait fait du président à Sagamore Hill. Il écrit: «Ma photo du président est formidable. Elle est tout à fait différente de toutes celles qui ont été faites avant et je crois que tous ceux qui le connaissent y verront une remarquable ressemblance. Je n'ai rien fait pour retoucher le visage et le montre lisse, avec son caractère bien à lui, sans rajouter quelque ligne que ce soit […] L'arrière-plan, les vêtements et tout le reste constituent comme une grande ombre, mettant ainsi le visage en évidence, dans toute sa rigueur; c'est la seule chose qu'on voit et je crois que c'est bien.» Cit. d'après Gidley 1998, p. 62.

11] C. T. Conover: «The monumental work of Edward S. Curtis», dans The Seattle Times, dimanche 21 juin 1953, p. 4–5.

12] Ibidem.

13] The Seattle Times, 15 novembre 1903.

14] Le mot potlach vient de la langue chinock et signifie «donner».

15] Curtis, The North American Indian, vol. XX, 1930, p. xvii.

16] C'est le cas par exemple d'une collection de 100

clichés d'excellente qualité conservée aujourd'hui à la Public Library de New York et provenant sans doute du fond de Pierpont Morgan.

17] Le Studio Curtis procédait avec le plus grand soin à l'archivage des clichés. Les numéros de négatifs ont été parfois changés, comme on peut le constater sur certaines épreuves, dont le numéro a été gratté et remplacé.

18] Avec un tel travail manuel, il n'est pas étonnant que les volumes et portfolios I–XI, produits par la célèbre firme John Andrew & Son de Boston, soient très différents des volumes XII–XX, faits par l'entreprise Suffolk Engraving & Electrotyping Co., également à Boston, mais dont le travail est nettement moins parfait. Les illustrations, et notamment la couleur d'impression, sont d'une tout autre qualité; ainsi, le marron est sensiblement plus clair à partir du volume XII. Les couleurs sont moins saturées, les noirs moins profonds.

19] Dans un catalogue de vente non daté du Studio Curtis, paru sans doute vers 1907 et plusieurs fois réédité avec de légères variantes jusque vers 1918, figurent ces indications avec les dimensions des photos données en pouces (inch): Epreuves «Small, from 6 1/2 x 8 1/2 plates, $ 3.00; Intermediate, from 14 x 17 plates, $ 15.00; Large, from 18 x 22 plates, $ 20.00.» Il n'est pas mentionné s'il s'agit de gravures ou d'épreuves gélatino-argentiques, mais la seconde hypothèse semble plus probable. A partir de 1909, le catalogue contient un texte à propos des cadres des photos: «Exclusive frames especially designed and toned to harmonize with the Indian studies can be purchased at prizes ranging from $ 2.50 each up».

20] Curtis indique les prix suivants: «8 x 10, framed [encadré], $ 10.00; 11 x 14, framed, $ 15.00; 14 x 17, framed, $ 30.00; 18 x 22, framed, $ 50.00. No Curt-tònes sold unframed. Crating and packing shipments $ 1.00.»

21] George Catlin, Letters and Notes on the North American Indians. Edité et commenté par Michael M. Mooney. New York: Gramercy Books, 1975. 1ère éd.: Londres, 1841.

22] Ibidem, p. 1.

23] Page imprimée d'origine inconnue, dans Oregonian, réimpression non datée. University of Washington, Special Collection Library, Sign. 484/2/8.

24] «The book represents an outlay of a million and a half dollar». Annonce de la conférence Curtis par Charles Rice, manager de Entertainment Tour, New York (en rapport avec la comédie musicale de Henry F. Gilbert). Cf. University of Washington, Special Collection Library, Sign. N 970.1 C94w.

25] Anonyme: «A Seattle Man's Triumph», dans The Seattle Sunday Times, suppl. magazine, 22 mai 1904, p. 2.

26] Andrews: «He knew the Red Man: Edward S. Curtis, photographer», dans The Magazine of Western History, Montana (Helena, MA), vol. 14, n° 2, April 1964, p. 5.

27] Lettre de Matilda Cox Stevenson, Smithsonian Institution, Bureau of American Ethnology, Washington D.C., 15 mars 1905.

28] Curtis, The North American Indian, vol. IV, 1909, p. 4.

Acknowledgements

The author and publisher would like to thank everyone who has been involved in this work. We are especially indebted to the Lower Saxony State and University Library in Göttingen, and to Mr Helmut Rohlfing, head of the rare books and manuscripts department there. They granted us access to copy No. 8, held by them, of Edward Curtis' encyclopaedia *The North American Indian*. The work was donated to the library by John Pierpont Morgan, a former student of the University of Göttingen.

Key information was provided to us by Verna Curtis of the Department of Photographs at the Library of Congress in Washington, which holds the largest collection of vintage prints by Edward Curtis. Our gratitude is expressed also to Julia van Haaften of New York Public Library and to Kristin Kinsey of the Special Collections of the University of Washington Libraries in Seattle. Finally, we are grateful to Lois Flury, who made available to us the extensive collection of her Seattle gallery, which specializes in Curtis' pictures. Without the kind and generous support of the above-named people and institutions, this book would never have come to fruition.

Danksagung

Verlag und Autor danken allen, die an diesem Werk mitgewirkt haben. Der Niedersächsischen Staats- und Universitätsbibliothek in Göttingen und Herrn Helmut Rohlfing, dem Leiter der Abteilung für seltene Bücher und Handschriften, gilt unser besonderer Dank. Sie gewährten uns Zugang zum Exemplar Nr. 8 der Enzyklopädie *The North American Indian* von Edward Curtis. John Pierpont Morgan – einst Student der Universität Göttingen – schenkte der Bibliothek das Werk.

Im Department of Photographs der Library of Congress in Washington, das die größte Sammlung an Vintage Prints von Edward Curtis besitzt, gab uns Verna Curtis wichtige Hinweise. Dank gebührt außerdem Julia van Haaften von der New York Public Library sowie Kristin Kinsey von den Special Collections der University of Washington Libraries in Seattle. Auch Lois Flury, die uns die reichhaltige Sammlung ihrer auf Curtis' Bilder spezialisierten Galerie in Seattle geöffnet hat, möchten wir an dieser Stelle unseren Dank aussprechen. Ohne die Unterstützung der genannten Personen und Institutionen hätte dieses Buch nicht realisiert werden können.

Remerciements

L'éditeur et l'auteur remercient tous ceux qui ont participé à la réalisation de cet ouvrage. Notre reconnaissance va tout spécialement à la Staats- und Universitätsbibliothek de Göttingen, en Basse-Saxe, et au responsable du département des manuscrits et livres rares, Monsieur Helmut Rohlfing, grâce à qui nous avons pu avoir accès à l'exemplaire n° 8 de l'encyclopédie *The North American Indian* d'Edward Curtis. John Pierpont Morgan – ancien étudiant de l'Université de Göttingen – avait fait don de ce livre à la bibliothèque.

Au Department of Photographs de la Library of Congress à Washington, qui détient la plus grande collection de Vintage Prints d'Edward Curtis, Verna Curtis a su nous donner d'importants renseignements. Nous remercions en outre Julia van Haaften de la New York Public Library ainsi que Kristin Kinsey des Special Collections de la University of Washington Libraries à Seattle. Que soit également remercié ici Lois Flury qui nous a ouvert à Seattle l'abondante collection de sa galerie, spécialisée en photos de Curtis. Sans le soutien des personnes et institutions nommées, ce livre n'aurait pu voir le jour.

Front cover: Sitting Bear. Arikara, 1908
Back cover: A Nakoaktok Chief's Daughter, 1914
Page 2: Edward S. Curtis, 1899

© 2006 by TASCHEN GmbH

This 2006 edition published by Barnes & Noble, Inc. by arrangement with TASCHEN GmbH.

Original edition:
© 1999 Benedikt Taschen Verlag GmbH

Edited by Hans Christian Adam, Göttingen
in collaboration with Ute Kieseyer, Cologne

Typography and Cover design:
Sense / Net, Andy Disl and Birgit Reber, Cologne

English translation by Malcolm Green, Heidelberg
French translation by Catherine Henry, Nancy

ISBN-13: 978-0-7607-8365-8
ISBN-10: 0-7607-8365-9

Printed in China

1 3 5 7 9 10 8 6 4 2 1